Pensions and Informal Sector in India

This book deals with the pension of uncovered people in India, the informal or unorganised sector workers who contribute more than 50% of India's total output. Until recently, these workers don't get any old-age security when they retire unlike those from the organised sector workers such as govt. employees or corporates. This book offers insights on the pension system of the informal sector in India.

This book is the outcome of field research of two years and the field research was conducted on MSME sector (a sub sector of unorganised sector), which provides the knowledge about the present state of the unorganised sector workers in MSMEs, their financial condition and stress, their work participation, their awareness level of old-age financial security or pension and their financial behaviour regarding pension savings in India. This book empirically demonstrates a relationship between financial literacy and willingness to save for retirement benefits among the informal sector workers in India. Access to banking also improves the probability of retirement savings along with the gender and education.

By reading this book, readers can understand the demographic change India is going to witness within the next 30 years and its challenges to meet the longevity risk of these workers.

Amlan Ghosh is Associate Professor in Finance at the Department of Management Studies, National Institute of Technology Durgapur, India. His research interest is financial public policy and mainly in the areas of pension sector, insurance sector, banking financial development, financial inclusion, MFIs and post offices.

Pensions and Informal
Sector in India

Amlan Ghosh

Routledge
Taylor & Francis Group
LONDON AND NEW YORK

First published 2023
by Routledge
4 Park Square, Milton Park, Abingdon, Oxon OX14 4RN

and by Routledge
605 Third Avenue, New York, NY 10158

Routledge is an imprint of the Taylor & Francis Group, an informa business

British Library Cataloguing-in-Publication Data
A catalogue record for this book is available from the British Library

Library of Congress Cataloging-in-Publication Data
Names: Ghosh, Amlan, author.
Title: Pensions and informal sector in India / Amlan Ghosh.
Description: First Edition. | New York, NY : Routledge, 2023. |
Includes bibliographical references and index. |
Identifiers: LCCN 2022014392 | ISBN 9781032307725 (hardback) |
ISBN 9781032307732 (paperback) | ISBN 9781003306573 (ebook)
Subjects: LCSH: Old age pensions—India. | Social security—India. |
Informal sector (Economics)—India. | Working poor—India—
Economic conditions.
Classification: LCC HD7105.35.I5 G46 2023 | DDC
331.25/20954—dc23/eng/20220502
LC record available at https://lccn.loc.gov/2022014392

ISBN: 9781032307725 (hbk)
ISBN: 9781032307732 (pbk)
ISBN: 9781003306573 (ebk)

DOI: 10.4324/9781003306573

Typeset in Times New Roman
by codeMantra

This book is dedicated to my parents.

Contents

Figures

Tables

Preface

India, presently, with the maximum young population, is going to have a high proportion of the elderly population in the coming years. The country, therefore, will face a huge challenge to provide old-age security to its working class in advancing years besides issues regarding employment. Ninety-three percent of India's workforce is employed in the informal or unorganised sector, and they are not covered under any formal retirement schemes or pension products. Although the informal sector accounts for a major share in the GDP, a considerable portion of its workers is more inclined towards poverty. Considering this situation, the Government of India introduced a Defined Contribution (DC) voluntary pension scheme (under NPS) for the unorganised sector. However, the participation to these schemes is relatively low.

To contemplate the connection between monetary proficiency (financial behaviour) and retirement planning for their old-age security (longevity risk) of the informal/unorganised sector in India, a project has been initiated in 2019 and carried out on the basis of a primary survey on the Ministry of Micro, Small & Medium Enterprises (MoMSME) recognised working-class populace in the unorganised sector of the state West Bengal (WB), India. The project aims to contribute to the existing knowledge base on the old-age financial planning of the unorganised sector workers in India and explores the financial stress of the workers and the social-economic factors impacting their pension financial planning.

This project was sponsored by the Impactful Policy Research in Social Science (IMPRESS) scheme of the Ministry of Human Resource Development (now Ministry of Education), Government of India, and supported by the Indian Council of Social Science Research (ICSSR), New Delhi, which aims to encourage social science research in policy-relevant areas so as to provide vital inputs in policy formulation, implementation and evaluation. The project was implemented at the National Institute of Technology Durgapur, West Bengal.

Dissemination of the findings of the project work to various stakeholders was the main motivating factor to write this book. This book is going to cover the existing pension system in India and its coverage. The content of this book is going to improve the overall understanding of the old-age financial planning of the informal/unorganised sector workers in the country for further research and policy analysis. Policymakers, researchers and students will find this book particularly useful.

Acknowledgements

I am thankful for the financial support from the Ministry of Education under the IMPRESS scheme to highlight old-age security of the informal/unorganised sector workers and their pension financial planning in India. I am particularly grateful for the cooperation extended by the ICSSR (Indian Council of Social Science Research) during the course of project implementation. ICSSR have been cooperative with all possible support during the Covid-19 pandemic.

The findings and interpretations, views and policy recommendations articulated here are personal and do not necessarily reflect the views of ICSSR or the Ministry of Education, New Delhi, India.

Abbreviations

AB-PMJAY Ayushman Bharat-Pradhan Mantri Jan Arogya Yojana
APY   Atal Pension Yojana
BPL   Below Poverty Line
CAG   Comptroller and Auditor General
CMIE   Centre for Monitoring Indian Economy
DB   Defined Benefit
DC   Defined Contribution
EDLIS   Employees' Deposit Linked Insurance Scheme
EPFO   Employee Provident Fund Organization
EPFS   Employees' Provident Fund Scheme
EPS   Employees' Pension Scheme
ESIC   Employees' State Insurance Corporation
GDP   Gross Domestic Product
GPF   General Provident Fund
GVA   Gross Value Added
IGNDPS   Indira Gandhi National Disability Pension Scheme
IGNOAPS   Indira Gandhi National Old Age Pension Scheme
IGNWPS   Indira Gandhi National Widow Pension Scheme
ILO   International Labour Organisation
IPOP   Integrated Programme for Older Persons
IRDAI   Insurance Regulatory and Development Authority
LICI   Life Insurance Corporation of India
MCGPI   Mercer CFA Institute Global Pension Index
MoF   Ministry of Finance
MoL   Ministry of Labour
MoL&E   Ministry of Labour and Employment
MoMSME   Ministry of Micro, Small & Medium Enterprises
MoSPI   Ministry of Statistics and Programme Implementation
MSME   Micro, Small & Medium Enterprises
NAS   National Accounts Statistics

NCEUS	National Commission for Enterprises in the Un-organised Sector
NDUW	National Database of Unorganised Workers
NFBS	National Family Benefit Scheme
NGO	Non-Governmental Organisation
NICE	National Initiative on Care for Elderly
NOAP	National Old Age Pension
NPHCE	National Programme for the Health Care for the Elderly
NPOP	National Policy for Older Persons
NPS	National Pension System
NSAP	National Social Assistance Programme
NSAP	National Social Assistance Programme
NSS	National Sample Survey
OASIS	Old Age Social and Income Security
OECD	Organisation for Economic Co-operation and Development
OOPE	Out-of-Pocket-Expenditure
PAYG	Pay-As-You-Go
PFM	Pension Fund Managers
PFRDA	Pension Fund Regulation and Development Authority
PLFS	Periodic Labour Force Survey
PMJDY	Pradhan Mantri Jan Dhan Yojana
PM-SYM	Pradhan Mantri Shram Yogi Maan-dhan Yojana
POP	Point of Presence
PPF	Public Provident Fund
RBI	Reserve Bank of India
SEWA	Self Employed Women Association
SHG	Self Help Group
SSA	Sarva Shiksha Abhiyan
UN	United Nations
UNFPA	United Nations Population Fund
UTI	Unit Trust of India
UWSSA	Unorganised Workers' Social Security Act
WPR	Worker Population Ratio
WWF	Working Women's Forum

1   Introduction

India is the second most populated country in the world with the maximum young population at present, and it is going to have a high proportion of the elderly population in the coming years. India, therefore, has the enormous responsibility of providing employment opportunities and stable income sources in the impending years along with providing old-age security and other security schemes such as providing food grains, livelihoods, poverty alleviation, and unemployment support. Access to retirement savings arrangements in India has traditionally been limited to the Central and State governments' salaried employees and larger private and public sector companies. Around 30 million central and state government employees (CMIE, 2021) are covered under a defined benefit pension program that is tax-funded and provides a 50% replacement wage at retirement. Public expenditure on pension and other retirement benefits of the Central Government alone is budgeted around INR 48 thousand crores (480 billion INR) in 2019–20 (MoF).

The major share of India's working population is employed in the informal or unorganised sector, which is excluded, until recently, from any admittance to formal retirement schemes or pension products. Indian economy is tangibly aware of the fact that there exists a vast employment in the informal or unorganised sector. India is estimated to have a total workforce of 45 crores (450 million); out of this, 93%, i.e., about 41.85 crores (418.5 million), of the working population are employed in the unorganised sector of the country (Economic Survey 2018–19). The agricultural sector employed almost 60% (246 million workers) of the unorganised sector employment. Around 4.4 crores (44 million) workers are engaged in construction work and the remaining are employed in manufacturing and service sectors.

The development of the informal or unorganised economy is a result of globalisation and the technological revolution, amongst other

DOI: 10.4324/9781003306573-1

factors (Castells, 1996). The concept of the informal or unorganised sector has been elusive as a category as well as an entity due to its mobility and lack of visibility. The informal sector workers in the economy along with the workers of the formal sector who are subject to formalisation within the formal economy are yet to accomplish fair labour standards. This has led to the re-conceptualising of informal sector work. With the expansion of the existing concept of informal work or informality by the International Labour Conference and International Conference of Labour Statistics in 2002 and 2003, respectively, advancement was witnessed in terms of improved accessibility and superiority of informal labour statistics.

The progress of total employment in India has always been higher than that of formal employment, demonstrating a faster employment growth rate in the informal sector. Existing data suggest that the share of informal/unorganised workers is increasing within the formal sector employment. For the last 20 years, India is currently into a state of *"informalisation of the formal sector"*, where the complete growth of organised sector employment has been informal in nature (NCEUS, 2009). The units of the unorganised sectors are generally unregistered and operate at low levels of organisation, generating employment and financial aid for most of the workforce. Labour relations in such units are based mostly on casual employment, kinship and social relations instead of written agreements with formal guarantees.

As home to one-fifth of the total world populace, the increase in formalisation in India has called for social security concerns for the unorganised sector workers, who spend their entire lives as casual labourers without any retirement security. With a notable growth in longevity and comparatively improved health care services, there has been a growth in the older people in India having more than 120 million elderly people and it is expected to increase to 324 million by 2050. India will have 21.16% of the population above the age of 60 compared to 60.34% aged between 15 and 59 years by 2050 (UN, 2019).

Significant contemplations for considering pension reforms in the unorganised sector in India were due to the absence of a nationwide social security framework, ageing population and social alteration because of the collapse of a customary family sustenance network. The principal reason for pensions is enabling of consumption and relieving life risk, reducing poverty and inequality between generations. With primitive disbursement and poor financial knowledge, these individuals face extensive difficulties settling on retirement arrangements. In spite of the fact that unorganised labourers may not "resign" similar to the workers in the organised segment, they have to plan for the inevitable decrease in procuring limit that will happen throughout old age, particularly because of their wellbeing.

Since 2001–02, various measures have been embraced by the Government of India for underlining the requirement for pension reforms for both Central Government and the unorganised sector for different reasons. Based on the recommendation of the project Old Age Social and Income Security Committee (OASIS), the Government of India began a determined pension reforms in 2004. The Government of India introduced the New Pension System (NPS) which replaces the old civil service pension scheme based on defined benefits (DB) with a new defined contribution (DC) scheme and created an interim Pension Fund Regulation and Development Authority (PFRDA). Later, the new NPS was offered to 400 plus million unorganised/informal sector workers in India. This makes the NPS an integrated pension system which is mandatory for government employees and voluntary for any workers. The Swavalamban Scheme was designed as a low-cost pension scheme and offered for the unorganised sector under the National Pension System.

The existing pension schemes available for organised sector employees in the government sectors and private sectors, along with the newly introduced NPS for the unorganised sector, could only cover 13.84% of the total working-age populace to give pay security during old age. Right around 86% of labourers work in the informal sectors of the economy and are compelled to survive on their own resources of income which they have saved, invested or inherited. In case of absence of such own resources due to lack of savings, the workers have to depend either on their children or on near relatives.

Pension reforms in India require individuals from the unorganised sector to decide whether to participate in pension funds or not and if they think of participating in the voluntary defined contribution pension schemes, how much to contribute. Another important aspect of investing in these pension schemes is their ability to deal with financial matters. Almost all the studies in developed and developing countries found that financial literacy has a positive causal and significant impact on the probability of participating in defied pension plans (Alessie et al., 2011; Fornero and Monticone, 2011; Klapper and Panos, 2011; Bucher-Koenen and Lusardi, 2011; Sekita, 2011). Studies also found that most individuals lack knowledge of basic concepts such as interest rates and inflation, and risk diversification (Almenberg and Säve-Söderbergh, 2011; Fornero and Monticone, 2011).

Financial literacy is quickly being perceived as centre aptitude in inexorably perplexing money-related conditions, and governments around the globe are investing all amounts of energy in improving money-related proficiency among their residents. Financial literacy studies build upon the infrastructure of economics education, both theoretical and empirical, in terms of subjects like savings, consumption, consumer choice (risk aversion, discount rates), economic environment (investment risks), and social security.

Evidence utilising the unit level family information recommends that essential money-linked assistance, such as investment, credit and instalments, can realise a noteworthy positive change in poor people's lives. Without satisfactory monetary education, it would be illogical to anticipate that people or family units should gauge the dangerous standard, which could be utilised as benchmarks for the monetary market.

The increasing level of dependency ratio creates a more fiscal burden on the economy, which ultimately impacts financial expenditures on social security measures. Therefore, it is key for the policymakers to study and comprehend the investment behaviour of the informal sector in the area of old-age securities in India. There are no such studies available to address this issue. Therefore, this work would be a modest attempt to address the following concern. The informal/unorganised sector workers constitute a large proportion of the working population who are without any old-age security or any social security cover in India. The informal sector contributes a significant share in the GDP, yet a substantial percentage of its workers is more inclined towards poverty. Considering this situation, the Government of India introduced a voluntary pension scheme for the informal sector based on Defined Contribution (DC). However, the penetration of this scheme is not as good as it was expected to be. Till March 2021, NPS could cover only 3.25 crores (32.5 million) workers from the unorganised sector under the umbrella of the formal pension for their old-age security. If we consider the situation in the percentage of unorganised sector, it is only 7.77% of the estimated 41.85 crores (418.5 million) unorganised sector workers. Therefore, almost 92% of unorganised sector workers are still out of any old-age security or protection (PFRDA, 2021).

To become a USD 5 trillion economy by 2024–25, India needs a sustainable real GDP growth of 8%. Experience from high-growth East Asian economies proposes that such a growth rate can only be achieved by a "virtuous cycle" of savings and investment supported by a favourable demographic phase. Improving investment in pension funds would improve the financial savings of the household sector along with the total savings of the economy. This would enhance the investment climate in the country for the long term as pension funds will be with more funds for a longer period of time.

Old-age social security is an essential tool in a welfare state, and one of its' main mechanisms is pension. In the case of developed countries, pensions are contributory and it is applicable to those who contribute for their own pension in old age. Whereas in the case of the developing countries, pensions are provided selectively and on a discretionary basis which ultimately reduces the overall coverage of pension. India, being a developing country, is no exception to this phenomenon and therefore has a low pension coverage.

2 Informal Sector in India

A little over 61% (2 billion) of global working population aged 15 and over work in the informal/unorganised sector. Half of the world's working population is employed informally in non-agricultural activities though the share of informal employment varies with regions. It is found that the degree of socio-economic development is positively related to the formality of the working population. Inevitably emerging and developing countries found to have substantially higher rates of informality than developed countries (ILO, 2018).

The unorganised sector is often described as the informal sector, although there exists a fine distinction between the two. The concept "informal" is more appropriate when we highlight a sector of employment (informal versus formal), whereas the term "unorganised" is suitable when we portray the employment conditions (regulated or unregulated) Kelles-Viitanen (1998). Even though the workers in the informal sector are mostly unorganised, the unorganised is not only found in the informal sector. Casual workers in the formal (i.e. organised) sector are a good example of the last category. Hence, workers without regulated employment conditions in the formal sector should also be considered as "unorganised" if we use the two terms interchangeably. The terms unorganised/ informal sector are used interchangeably in the Indian context.

The National Commission for Enterprises in the Unorganised Sector (NCEUS) was set up in 2004 by the Government of India to "review the status of unorganised/informal sector in India including the nature of enterprises, their size, spread and scope, and magnitude of employment". After extensive discussions and consultations, the Commission (NCEUS) has defined the unorganised sector in the following way: *"The unorganised/informal sector consists of all unincorporated private enterprises owned by individuals or households engaged in the sale and production of goods and services operated on a proprietary or partnership basis and with less than ten total workers"* (NCEUS, 2009).

DOI: 10.4324/9781003306573-2

NCEUS (2009) has mentioned that the unorganised sector consists of all unincorporated private enterprises owned by individuals or households engaged in the sale and production of goods and services operated on a proprietary or partnership basis and with less than ten total workers. The Unorganised Workers' Social Security Act, 2008, has defined the term "unorganised worker" as a home-based worker, self-employed worker or a wage worker in the unorganised sector and includes a worker in the organised sector without any contract or without other benefits such as paid leave, health aids or any old-age security. Any of the following Acts does not cover them: The Employee's Compensation Act, 1923, The Industrial Disputes Act, 1947, The Employee's State Insurance Act, 1948, The Employees Provident Funds and Miscellaneous Provision Act, 1952, The Maternity Benefit Act, 1961 and The Payment of Gratuity Act, 1972 (UWSSA, 2009).

2.1 Salient Characteristics of the Unorganised Sector and Employees

Indian unorganised sector mixes a heterogeneous mix of workers from self-employed individuals to farmers, from rickshaw pullers to vendors, from construction workers to labourers. The workers could be static or could be travelling to different parts of the nation for work in the formal or informal sector. From the viewpoint of means of production or economic activity, the salient characteristics of the unorganised/informal sector are as follows:

Scale of operation are typically small and employ less than ten workers;
Employment in this sector is seasonal in nature especially in agriculture/farm sector;
Employ low skill workers in labour intensive work;
This sector provides low real wages with poor working conditions;
A multitude of casual and contractual employment and no job security; Insufficient and futile labour laws;
Inadequate social security or no old age security for the workers;
Easier entry and exit than in the formal sector;
Usually require low level of capital investment;

Due to lack of formal education, skills and awareness, informal sector workers are unaware of their rights and have negligible negotiating power with their employers and intermediaries (ILO, 2000).

Thus, the unorganised sector has emerged as a source of low cost to employment to absorb India's vast unskilled and often under-educated labour force, which cannot be employed elsewhere. The recent development of the informal sector has unfavourably affected the employment and income security of the majority of the workforce in India. Due to low wages or income and poor working conditions, unorganised sector workers are usually subject to significant exploitation and indebtedness. There exists a positive relationship between informal employment and poverty. Any attempt to regulate this sector with a more effective legal and institutional framework may hinder the possibilities of labour absorbing capacity of this sector.

2.2 Broad Classification of the Unorganised Sector Employment

Employment in India can be implicitly clustered into four groups based on the quality and its sectoral association. These groups are (a) Formal employment in the formal or organised sector, (b) Informal employment in the formal sector, (c) Formal employment in the informal sector and (d) Informal employment in the informal sector (Ministry of Labour & Employment, 2015). The share of Informal employment in the unorganised sector is predominant in India.

Table 2.1 shows that the share of employment in the unorganised sector has increased almost by 4% and the share of organised sector employment reduced to 13.2% of the total employment scenario in India from 2011–12 to 2017–18. Importantly, Informal employment in the informal (unorganised) sector has increased by 2.9% during the same time. But there has been a marginal improvement in the formal sector also with 0.9% in the unorganised sector. This improvement may have been due to the more formalisation of works or redefining of the MSME sector in India. The share of informal workers in the organised sector also decreased by 4.6% from 2011–12 to 2017–18.

Table 2.1 Employment Distribution – Organised and Unorganised (in %)

Workers	2011–12			2017–18		
	Unorganised	Organised	Total	Unorganised	Organised	Total
Informal	82.6	9.8	92.4	85.5	5.2	90.7
Formal	0.4	7.2	7.6	1.3	7.9	9.3
Total	83.0	17.0	100	86.8	13.2	100

Source: NSS 68th unit level data on employment unemployment, 2011–12; Periodic Labour Force Survey, 2017–18; Murthy (2019).

India's Ministry of Labour (2008) classified the unorganised sector labour force in India into four categories by occupation, nature of employment, especially distressed categories and service categories. The unorganised occupational groups include small and marginal farmers, landless agricultural labourers, sharecroppers, fishermen, those engaged in animal husbandry, beedi rolling, labelling and packing, building and construction workers, leather workers, weavers, artisans, salt workers, workers in brick kilns and stone quarries, workers in sawmills and workers in oil mills. A separate category based on the nature of employment includes attached agricultural labourers, bonded labourers, migrant workers, contract and casual labourers. Additional separate category dedicated to distressed unorganised sector includes toddy tappers, scavengers, carriers of head loads, drivers of animal-driven vehicles, loaders and unloaders. The last unorganised labour category includes service workers such as midwives, domestic workers, barbers, vegetable and fruit vendors, newspaper vendors, pavement vendors, hand cart operators and unorganised retail (Table 2.2).

Table 2.2 Share of Labour Input in Unorganised Sector (in %)

Sl. No.	Category/Description	Share of Unorganised Sector 2004–05
1	Agriculture and forestry	99.9
2	Fishing	98.7
3	Mining	64.4
4	Manufacturing	87.7
5	Electricity, gas, watersupply	12.4
6	Construction	92.4
7	Wholesale and retail trade	98.3
8	Hotel and restaurants	96.7
9	Transport, storage and communication	82.2
10	Financial intermediation	32.4
11	Real estate, renting and business activities	81.4
12	Public administration and defence, etc.	2.6
13	Education	37.9
14	Health and social work	55.1
15	Other community, social and personal services	92.5
16	Private households with employed persons	100
17	Extra territorial organisations and bodies	87.8
	Grand total	93

Source: Report of the Committee on Unorganised Sector Statistics, 2012.

The unorganised sector plays a critical role in our economy in terms of employment opportunities for many working populations, thereby reducing poverty. A huge segment of the working population (87%) is in the unorganised sector, contributing a considerable share of the country's net domestic product. The employment generated by this sector is vital for savings and capital formation in the economy.

2.3 Gross Value Added and the Unorganised Sector in India

The Gross Value Added (GVA) is considered as an important determinant to measure the economic contribution of the unorganised sector towards the country. GVA can be explained as the value of services and goods produced in a place, sector or industry. Both GVA and GDP are utilised to measure the output of a country; hence both are vital in each other's calculation. Table 2.3 highlighted the contribution of organised and unorganised sectors to total GVA in India. The total share of the unorganised sector has been more than 50% of total GVA for the last decades and from 2011–12 to 2017–18, it followed the same trend with 52.4% contribution by the unorganised sector. In its report, the Committee on Unorganised Sector Statistic (NSC, 2012), the National Statistics Commission emphasised the importance of unorganised sector workforce in improving the country's GVA percentage.

2.4 Worker Population Ratio in India

In order to understand the extent of informal/unorganised employment in the country, information on diverse aspects of unorganised sector workers needs to be examined. The overall Worker Population Ratio (WPR) has been improved over the years in India (Table 2.4). At all India level, the percentage of workers for the age 15 and above is at 47.3% in 2018–19 (NSSO, 2019–20). The share of rural Indian workers is 5% more than the urban India in the age group of 15 years and above.

2.5 Worker Profile of Unorganised Sector Workers in Different Sectors of Economy

The Periodic Labour Force Survey (PLFS, 2020) report by the Ministry of Statistics and Programme Implementation finds that 68.4% of the workers in the non-agriculture sector are engaged with the informal sector. Among the regular wage/salaried workers in the

Table 2.3 Share of Formal/Informal Sectors across Broad Sectors to GVA (in %)

Industry	2011–12			2017–18		
	Organised/ Formal	Unorganised/ Informal	Total	Organised/ formal	Unorganised/ Informal	Total
Agriculture, forestry and fishing	3.2	96.8	100	2.9	97.1	100
Mining and quarrying	77.4	22.6	100	77.5	22.5	100
Manufacturing	74.5	25.5	100	77.3	22.7	100
Gas, water supply, electricity and other utility services	95.7	4.3	100	94.7	5.3	100
Construction	23.6	76.4	100	25.5	74.5	100
Accommodation and food services, repair, trade	13.4	86.6	100	13.4	86.6	100
Transport, storage, communication and services related to broadcasting	53.0	47.0	100	52.3	47.7	100
Financial services	90.7	9.3	100	88.1	11.9	100
Real estate, ownership of dwelling and professional services	36.9	63.1	100	47.2	52.8	100
Public administration and defense	100.0	0.0	100	100.0	0.0	100
Other services	58.8	41.2	100	52.1	47.9	100
Total GVA (at basic prices)	46.1	53.9	100	47.6	52.4	100

Table 2.4 Worker Population Ratio (WPR)
by Region & Gender (in %)

	2017–18	2018–19
All-India		
All gender and all-ages	34.7	35.3
Age 15 and above	46.8	47.3
Urban		
All gender and all-ages	33.9	34.1
Age 15 and above	43.9	43.9
Rural		
All gender and all-ages	35	35.8
Age 15 and above	48.1	48.9

WPR (worker population ratio): The percentage
of employed persons in the population.

non-agriculture sector (of the informal sector), 69.5% had no written job contract, 53.8% were not eligible for paid leave and 51.9% are not eligible for any social security benefits. According to the Ministry of Labour and Employment's report (Employment in Informal Sector and Condition of Informal Employment of 2015), 82% of those employed in agriculture (minus crop and animal husbandry) and the non-agriculture sector had no written job contract, 77.3% got no paid leave and 69% were not eligible for any social security benefits.

The majority of the Indian labour force or workers are uneducated or under-educated, which can be inferred from the educational data about the workers (Table 2.5). By the end of 1999–2000, almost 50% of the labour force had below primary school level education. However, with the implementation of the SSA programme by the Government in early 2000, this trend has been declining over time with increasing educational attainment; and by 2011–12, the share of below primary school level education had fallen to 43% and by 2021 it has come down to 24% which is quite commendable. At present, almost 65% workforce is having up to higher secondary level education.

If we study the sectoral distribution of employment of the unorganised sector in India across different sectors, we may witness the impact of low literacy in the job assignments too. Construction and manufacturing were the highest non-agricultural employment sector for the under-educated workers in India, with 46% of employment in 2011–12. In the post liberalised era, when the economy was open, and investments were coming, the construction and services sector was improving rapidly and evolved as the key employer in the non-agricultural sector (Figure 2.1). During 2011–12, the service sector (THTC and

Table 2.5 Population above 15 Years of Age: By Education Level

All India

Year	All Education Groups	No Education	Primary (up to V)	Secondary (VI–IX)	Higher Secondary (XI–XII)	≥ Graduate
1999–2000	**100%**	**24%**	**24%**	**20%**	**21%**	**11%**
2010–11	**100%**	**22%**	**21%**	**18%**	**21%**	**18%**
2016–17	96,45,03,331	20,61,87,632	19,31,57,037	19,66,62,847	26,62,53,993	10,22,41,822
(In %)	**100%**	**21%**	**20%**	**20%**	**28%**	**11%**
2017–18	98,74,60,847	10,88,19,827	26,27,61,530	21,47,31,266	29,94,59,106	10,16,89,118
(In %)	**100%**	**11%**	**27%**	**22%**	**30%**	**10%**
2018–19	1,01,10,21,610	4,13,40,661	31,79,62,433	22,88,18,476	31,93,16,277	10,35,83,762
(In %)	**100%**	**4%**	**31%**	**23%**	**32%**	**10%**
2019–2020	**1,03,52,70,203**	**1,88,24,028**	**33,73,83,373**	**23,54,40,534**	**34,06,81,146**	**10,29,41,122**
(In %)	**100%**	**2%**	**33%**	**23%**	**33%**	**10%**
2020–21	1,06,00,92,260	4,61,44,164	20,99,51,743	29,43,85,700	40,96,86,923	9,99,23,729
(In %)	**100%**	**4.35%**	**19.81%**	**27.77%**	**38.65%**	**9.43%**

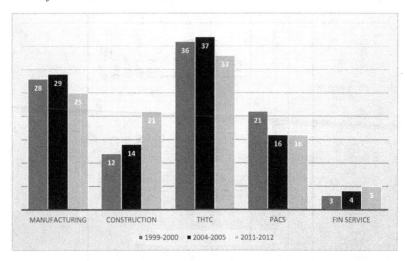

Figure 2.1 Sectoral Distribution of Total Unorganised Sector Employment.
Source: NSS-EUS (various issues)
Note: THTC – Trade, Hotels, Transport and Communication, FIN service – Financial Services, Insurance and Real Estate, PACS – Public Administration, Community Services.

Table 2.6 Employed Persons: By Major Industry Groups

All India

Year	Agriculture (%)	Industry (%)	Services (%)	Not Classified Elsewhere (%)	Total (%)
2016–17	36.90	29.94	32.93	0.23	100
2017–18	36.05	27.59	36.22	0.13	100
2018–19	36.25	25.88	37.70	0.16	100
2019–20	36.77	25.69	37.48	0.06	100
2020–21	39.71	23.34	36.92	0.03	100

Source: CMIE-Economic Outlook (2021).

FIN Service) and construction sector together generated 42% of the total non-agricultural jobs in India.

The trend for the service sector continues in the recent past also. The contribution of the service sector has improved considerably in the total GDP of India, and the same industry contributes almost 37% of the total employment in India in 2019–20 (Table 2.6). The service sector and industry in India generate more than 60% of the total employment in the Indian economy. Importantly, the share of employment in the agriculture sector has increased recently to almost 40%, but agriculture's overall contribution is 17.8% of our GDP (Economic Survey, 2021). About 53.2% of the male workers and 71.1% of the female workers were engaged in the agricultural sector during 2018–19. At the same time, 68.4% of the workers in the non-agriculture sector were employed in the informal sector in India (PLFS, 2020).

2.6 Employment Conditions of Workers in the Informal Sector

The recent annual report of the Periodic Labour Force Survey (PLFS) (2020) for the year 2018–19, by the Ministry of Statistics and Programme Implementation, Govt. of India, highlighted the employment condition of the non-agricultural sector workers in India. The survey finds that more than 70% of the workers in the non-agricultural sector in India do not have any written job contract in the employment, which makes them vulnerable to a steady income in their job. Almost 54% of the regular wage/salaried employees are not eligible for any paid leave which they could avail during sickness or maternity, etc. They can avail such leaves only with the loss of pay. More than half of the regular workers (51.9%) were not eligible for any sort of social security benefit such as health care or maternity benefits, gratuity, PF/pension (i.e., GPF, CPF, PPF, pension), etc. (Table 2.7).

Table 2.7 Employee Status in Non-Agriculture Sector

Category	Percentage of Regular Wage/Salaried Employees Who Had No Written Job Contract		Percentage of Regular Wage/Salaried Employees Not Eligible for Paid Leave		Percentage of Regular Wage/Salaried Employees Not Eligible for Any Social Security Benefit	
	PLFS (2018–19)	*PLFS (2018–19)*	*PLFS (2018–19)*	*PLFS (2018–19)*	*PLFS (2018–19)*	*PLFS (2018–19)*
Male	70.3	72.3	54.7	55.2	51.2	49.0
Female	66.5	66.8	50.6	50.4	54.4	51.8
Person	69.5	71.1	53.8	54.2	51.9	49.6

Source: Periodic Labour Force Survey (PLFS) (2020).

3 Pension in India

3.1 Pension System

Pension is a financial product that assures the old-age financial security when people are not physically fit to earn their living. These are generally monthly instalments of payments made on superannuation to any individual for his/her living post-retirement or after attaining certain age (60/65 years) depending on the age of retirement or policy. The prime objective of the pension is consumption smoothing so that individuals can maintain living or minimum consumption at old age when their steady income stops at regular interval due to retirement. The flow of pension at regular interval helps beneficiaries to overcome against longevity and inflation risks.

There is a long debate about the types of pensions that should prevail in the economy. Whether the pension benefit should be defined (unfunded) or the pension should be based on contribution. By the types of pensions here, it means whether defined benefit (DB) or defined contribution (DC). Both have their own advantages and disadvantages, but the implementation of any such types needs to be evaluated based on individual countries' demographic characteristics, requirements, economic conditions and sustainability. The objective of the pension plans should be on overall household welfare and the accessible pack of services to the elderly (Barr, 2002).

In DB pension scheme, the benefit is predefined, and the worker does not need to contribute to having pension for their old age. In contrast, in the DC pension scheme, the benefit depends on the total contribution by the employer and the employee and the net interest earned on it. Consequently, the responsibility of the pension in the defined benefit falls on the employer or the state while the same shift to the worker in the defined contribution pension scheme.

DOI: 10.4324/9781003306573-3

The three broad categories of pension have been mentioned in the World Bank document (1994), First Pillar, Second Pillar and Third Pillar, with each pillar having different objectives.

The first pillar is intended to provide old-age security to all elderly, comparable to any state-funded mandatory social security scheme targeted at low-income people. These schemes run as Pay-As-You-Go (PAYG) Schemes where the present working populations are subsidising the retirement payment of the older generation and supported by the state from the general tax revenue. Since these schemes are non-contributory, therefore it is risk-free for the beneficiaries and prevalent worldwide. Since the state funds the Scheme, it has a fiscal ramification, and many states/Governments are shifting focus from DB to contributory schemes (DC; Table 3.1).

The second pillar is the occupational pension schemes, mainly to supplement first-pillar pension benefits, for the workers where a fund is generated and preserved by the employer to buy an annuity for providing pension with the mandatory contribution of employees/workers on wages. Therefore, these schemes provide more benefits to those who contribute more to the pension fund (PF). These schemes are classified as:

Defined Benefit (DB) schemes where the pension benefit is predefined as a percentage of the salary of the employee. In these schemes, the employer/state who is the pension sponsor bears the investment risk. DB Schemes are attractive and beneficial to the employees. However, it directly impacts the fiscal budget of the state and the liability of the state increases at times of economic crisis.

Defined Contribution (DC) Schemes in which contributions are explicitly defined but the benefits are linked to the actual return from the investment made by the fund houses who manage the fund on behalf of the employees or workers. The fund houses invest the corpus in the market, and the return depends on the market performance. The investors, i.e., beneficiaries, bear the investment risks in the market. Since the risk shifts from employer/state to employee/workers,

Table 3.1 World Bank Pension Framework 1994

Category	Funding Type	Scheme Type
Pillar I	Non-contributory	Social security schemes or basic pension.
Pillar II	Contributory (forced savings)	Occupational pension schemes
Pillar III	Contributory (voluntary savings)	Individual private pension

Source: World Bank (1994), Willmore (2000).

there has been a worldwide alteration towards DC schemes from DB schemes. However, the success of these DC schemes would depend on efficient fund management and asset allocation in dynamic economic conditions.

The third pillar schemes are meant for the unorganised sector workers or employees and the self-employed who are not covered by any employee-managed pension schemes. These schemes are also subscribed to by organised-sector employees deploying additional funds to improve pension inflows. These are contributory pension schemes which mean employees or workers are need to sponsor themselves to save for their old-age security, and the savings of these schemes would be managed by the Pension Fund houses which will invest the same in the market to create the fund for the savers or the beneficiaries'.

The World Bank favours privately run second-pillar schemes because governments are likely to interfere in the investment decisions of PFs for political ends rather than based on economic efficiency, thus using inefficiently "captive" resources. Currently, the World Bank promotes a five-pillar system for post-retirement protection. This kind of framework is sometimes used to define PF architecture. The five pillars are – Pillar Zero: non-contributory social pension and assistance (universal or means-tested) for poverty alleviation; Pillar One: a publicly managed, tax-financed social safety net; Pillar Two: a mandatory, privately managed, fully funded contribution scheme; Pillar Three: voluntary personal savings and insurance; and Pillar Four: informal support (e.g. family support), other formal social programs (e.g. health care and housing), and other individual financial and non-financial assets (e.g. homeownership and reverse mortgage where available).

3.2 Pension in India

In India, the old-age pension scheme can be traced back to 1881 when the Royal Commission on Civil Establishments started giving pension benefits to government employees during British rule. Since then, the concept of pension was incepted. With the advent of time, the Indian Government Acts made further provisions in 1919 and 1935. Schemes like General Provident Fund (GPF) under Workmen Compensation Act, 1923 was launched followed by Coal Mines Provident Fund Scheme in 1945 for the coal mine employee. After the independence, the policymakers were focusing more on the welfare of the employees than the proper management of the system or sustainability of the programmes. Therefore, these schemes were later consolidated and expanded to provide retirement benefits to the entire public sector working population. Several provident funds were also set up after independence to extend coverage among the private sector, such as Employees' Provident Fund Scheme (EPFS) 1952, Assam Tea Plantation EPFS in 1955, Employees' Pension Fund Scheme in 1955, Jammu and Kashmir Employees' Provident Funds Act, 1961 and the Seamen's Provident Fund Act, 1966 (Goswami, 2001).

Pension coverage in India has mainly been financed through employer and employee participation. As a result, the major retirement benefits are mostly been restricted to the organised sector which constitutes about 13% of the total working population. Rest 87% workers who are in unorganised sector are not covered under the ambit of any social security system.

3.3 Social Security System in India

Indian social security for old-age people has the following schemes which are custom made and directed to deliver benefits to some specific sectors and few schemes are for general people in different needs. Mainly, India has the following discussed schemes to benefit its people.

1 The civil service schemes,
2 The employee provident fund organization (EPFO),
3 The Scheme of public enterprises,
4 Superannuation plans of the corporate sector,
5 Voluntary tax advantaged schemes,
6 Social assistance schemes and
7 Micro-pension schemes.

3.3.1 The Civil Service Schemes

The central government, union territories and state governments, and autonomous institutions, local public bodies (backed by a government guarantee) provide pension benefits to the employees. The central government administers separate pension programs for civil service employees, Indian railways employees, Indian defence staff and the post and telecommunications departments. These pension schemes are typically non-contributory and run on a defined-benefit basis.

Central, state and local government employees are covered under a civil service scheme, which receives three types of retirement supports. First, the civil service receives an unfunded DB pension indexed for price and has relatively generous and commutation provision and survivor benefit. Second, each employee is mandated to contribute a percentage of his salary to government provident fund scheme. Lastly, civil servant also receives a lump sum gratuity benefit based on the year of service and salary level where the maximum ceiling is Rs. 35 lakhs. The entire pension expenditure is charged in the annual revenue expenditure account of the government. The combined expenditure of central and state governments on pension and other retirement benefits was Rs. 413, 435 crore, i.e., Rs. 4,134 billion in 2017–18 (MoF, 2019). Private sector workers were not under any DB programmes for their old-age security. They are getting the benefit of the provident fund only after the creation of EPFO.

3.3.2 The Employee Provident Fund Organization (EPFO)

The EPFO is an autonomous body under the Ministry of Labour & Employment (MoL&E), Government of India. EPFO administers the Employees' Provident Funds and Miscellaneous Provisions Act, 1952. The Act applies to a defined class of industries where 20 or more workers are employed.

The following three schemes have been framed under the Act:

i   The Employees' Provident Funds Scheme, 1952 (EPF) – (w.e.f. 1 November 1952)
ii The Employees' Pension Scheme, 1995 (EPS) (w.e.f 16 November 1995) [replacing the Employees' Family Pension Scheme, 1971]
iii The Employees' Deposit Linked Insurance Scheme, 1976 (EDLI) – (w.e.f. 1 August 1976).

The covered organisations are required to comply the Act statutorily in respect of all their employees who are drawing wages up to Rs. 15,000 per month (w.e.f. 1 August 1976) which was revised from the previous wage ceiling of Rs. 6,500 in 2014. Provident Fund is based on a DC scheme where both the employees and the employers contribute their mandated share. A mix of "defined contribution" and "defined benefit" forms the Pension Scheme. The employees do not have to contribute to this scheme. Insurance scheme is a deposit linked Scheme that provides for benefits up to Rs. 600,000/- without any contribution from employees.

EPFO is one of the World's largest social security providers with 6.91 million pensioners as on 2020–21. The benefits admissible under each of the three schemes are indicated in Table 3.2.

The rate of contribution payable to PF by the employees and the employers under the Act has been revised timely by the finance ministry.

Table 3.2 The Benefits Admissible under EPF, EPS and EDLI Schemes

The Employees' Provident Funds Scheme (EPF)	The Employees' Pension Scheme (EPS)	The Employees' Deposit Linked Insurance Scheme (EDLI)
Accumulated fund plus interest upon retirement, resignation, death. Partial withdrawals allowed for specific expenses such as higher education, marriage, house construction, illness etc.	Monthly pension for members on superannuation/ retirement, disability. Monthly pension for dependents of deceased member viz. widow(er), children, parent / nominee. Past service benefit to participants of erstwhile Family Pension Scheme, 1971	The benefits are provided in case of death of an employee who was member of the Scheme at the time of death. For service less than 12 months, insurance benefit up to Rs. 1 Lacs is paid. For continuous service of 12 months in the same establishment, insurance benefit from Rs. 2.5 Lacs to Rs. 6 Lacs is paid

Source: EPFO Annual Reports (various years).

It was last modified in 1997 and presently, the rate of contribution excluding the administrative charges and contribution in the EDLI scheme is 12% on the wages both for employer as well as the employee. The employer needs to bear the entire administrative charges for EPF and contribution under EDLI scheme. The Government of India contributes 1.16% of the total wages to the EPS (Table 3.3).

3.3.2.1 Development and Performance of EPFO

At the time of launch, the maximum wage ceiling for joining the EPF schemes was Rs. 300 per month which now has been revised at Rs. 15,000 per month in 2014 by the finance ministry based on the improved wages in the economy and larger extension of social security schemes to the workers. This has a direct impact on the coverage of more organisations and the growth of subscribers in EPF and EPS schemes. The total number of establishment registered with the EPFO is 1.59 million at the end of the financial year 2020–21. During the last five years, the number of establishment has increased from 0.926 million in 2015–16 to 1.59 million in 2020–21 (Figure 3.1).

The last five years have witnessed a phenomenal growth in the number of subscribers of EPFO. This growth was primarily caused due to change in the regulations by the finance ministry on the maximum

Table 3.3 Rate of Contribution in EPFO

	Contribution Accounts (Rate of Contribution)			Administration Accounts (Rate of Contribution)		Total
	EPF	EPS	EDLI	EPF	EDLI	
Employer	3.67	8.33	0.5	0.5	0	13
Employee	12	0	0	0	0	12
Central Government	0	1.16	0	0	0	1.16
Total	15.67	9.49	0.5	0.5	0	26.16

Source: EPFO Annual Report (2020–21).

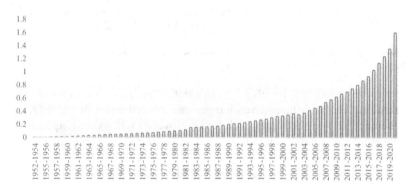

Figure 3.1 Number of Establishment in EPFO since Inception (in millions).
Source: EPFO Annual Reports (1952–2021).

wage ceiling for joining the EPF in 2014 along with the increased awareness among the people about the old-age security and willingness to register with the EPFO. The number of subscribers has increased from 158.4 million in 2014–15 to 258.7 million in 2020–21 (Figure 3.2).

The EPFO, with the consent of the finance ministry, decides the rate of interest for the EPF scheme every year and the rate of interest is dependent on the macro economic and financial market conditions. The rate of interest for the FY 2020–21 is 8.5%. The receipts and corpus have continuously grown due to increase in the subscribers along with the increase in basic wage rates in India. The growth in the receipts and corpus in the last five years is as below (Table 3.4).

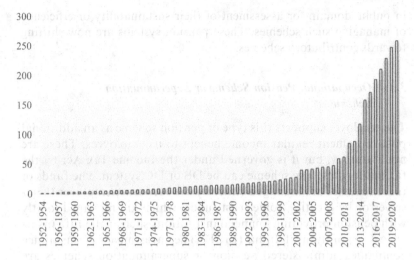

Figure 3.2 Number of Subscriber in EPFO since Inception (in million).
Source: EPFO Annual Reports (1952–2021).

Table 3.4 Pension Fund Receipts & Corpus (in crore)

Year	Contribution (Employer's Share)	Contribution (Govt. Share)	Total Contribution Received During the Year	Interest	Corpus as at the End of Financial Year
2015–16	29,026.88	3,280.2	32,307.08	21,662.14	277,077.2
2016–17	32,108.65	4,284.8	36,393.45	25,381.19	318,412.38
2017–18	36,618.23	5,757.42	42,375.65	30,260.66	393,604.4
2018–19	40,259.74	6,401.9	46,661.64	32,982.68	437,762.54
2019–20	44,448.55	7,504.59	51,953.14	39,042.05	530,846.39
2020–21a	44,009.53	6,552.48	50,562.01	35,773.36	593,546.52

Source: EPFO Annual Report 2020–21.
aFigures are provisional.

3.3.3 *Public Sector Enterprises*

Public sector enterprises such as RBI, LICI, Public sector Banks, Public sector insurance companies, public sector oil companies or any other public sector organisations such as electricity boards, etc. have their own pension schemes which are, in general, contributory in nature. These schemes are administered and managed by individual enterprises. The design of such pension schemes is not well known or in public domain for assessment of their sustainability or efficiency of managing such schemes. These pension systems are now shifting towards contributory schemes.

3.3.4 Occupational Pension Scheme or Superannuation Scheme

The employer supports this type of pension scheme as an additional post-retirement regular income benefit to its employees. These are not statutory, but it is governed under the Income Tax Act by the tax authorities. The scheme can be DB or DC system. The funds of these schemes are managed either by the corporate/employer them-selves or by creating some trust funds, which are managed jointly with pension providing financial institutions such as the Life Insur-ance Corporation of India (LICI). The investments of insurance companies administered pension or superannuation schemes are regulated by the Insurance Regulatory and Development Authority (IRDAI) guidelines. However, the overall granting and supervisory authority are the Income Tax authorities (Asher, 2007). Neverthe-less, the mode of payment of pensions varies from enterprise to enterprise.

3.3.5 Voluntary Tax-Advantaged Saving Schemes

This kind of scheme comprises small saving schemes of central and state governments and group annuity schemes of life insurance companies. Interest rates on small savings financial instruments or schemes have traditionally been set at above market rate. This has two impacts on the savings behaviour. One, it encourages people to save at smaller denominations. Second, because of higher interest rates than the market, it has a negative impact on investments of other financial securities in capital markets such as mutual funds.

3.3.6 Social Assistance Schemes

The Directive Principles of State Policy, Article 41 of the Indian Con-stitution states that the State "to make effective provision, within the limits of its economic capacity, for public assistance in case of un-employment, sickness, old age, disablement and other cases of unde-served want". For economically weaker sections of people in India, several central and state government-run social assistance programs and welfare funds introduced at different times.

3.3.6.1 Central Schemes

The Government of India has taken certain policies for elderly (workers and non-workers) citizens such as Integrated Programme for Older Persons (IPOP) 1992; National Policy for Older Persons (NPOP) 1999; Maintenance and Welfare of Parents and Senior Citizen's Act, 2007; National Initiative on Care for Elderly (NICE) 2000; National Programme for the Health Care for the Elderly (NPHCE).

There are specific schemes which are there specially targeted the elderly in India under the National Social Assistance Programme (NSAP).

National Old Age Pension (NOAP) {renamed as Indira Gandhi National Old Age Pension Scheme (IGNOAPS) in 2007}, was launched by the Central Government on August 15, 1995, for persons below poverty line (BPL) who were aged 65 and above. The pension was created with the contribution of the central government (Rs. 200 per month) and a contribution from the state government, which may vary from state to state. The selection of the beneficiaries is made with the help of gram panchayats under the aegis of state government. In 2011, the contribution of the central government has increased to Rs. 500 for persons above 80 years leaving the state to decide their own contribution to implementing the scheme.

Indira Gandhi National Disability Pension Scheme (IGNDPS) was launched in February 2009 to provide social benefits to the poor household living BPL in the case of PWDs with the age group of 18–79 years and having 80% and above /multiple disabilities. Govt. of India fund Scheme where the beneficiaries receive Rs. 300/- per month under this scheme and this State Govt. is providing Rs. 200/- per month to each beneficiary under IGNDP.

The Indira Gandhi National Widow Pension Scheme (IGNWPS) was introduced in 2009 to assist widows who are living BPL in the age group 40–64 (later revised as 40–59) with a monthly pension of Rs. 200/- per month and the state governments may contribute at least an equal amount so that a beneficiary gets at least Rs. 400/- per month. After the beneficiaries attain the age of 60, they automatically qualify for pension under IGNOAPS.

The National Family Benefit Scheme (NFBS) provides central assistance in the form of lump-sum family benefits of Rs. 10,000 to the grieving household BPL in case of death of the primary breadwinner irrespective of the cause of death. This scheme applies to all the eligible persons in the age group of 18–64. Local enquiry determines the beneficiary from the surviving members of the deceased's household to provide financial assistance.

Annapurna Scheme was launched on 1 April 2000 by the Government of India, known as a new scheme to provide food security to those senior citizens who are not covered under any scheme of the NOAPS. Under the Annapurna Scheme, 10 kgs of food grains per month are provided free of cost to the beneficiary.

All the central government schemes mentioned above are operational in all the states. To date (June 2021), more than 336 crores. People have benefited under the National Social Assistance Programme (NSAP, 2021).

3.3.6.2 State Schemes

Apart from the central Government's schemes, several state governments have their own widow, disabled and old-age pension schemes with varying degrees of benefits and eligibility criteria. These schemes are funded from their own resources. It is important to note that several states have started their old-age security programmes earlier than the Central Government who initiated these schemes in the early 90s. States like Uttar Pradesh started their old-age pension scheme in 1957, and Andhra Pradesh (undivided) started as early as 1960. Table 3.5 highlights the year of introduction of old-age pension schemes, age criteria and the monthly pension amount in different states and union territories in India (Irudaya, 2008).

3.3.7 Micro-Pension Schemes

Micro-pension schemes are personal contributory retirement savings plans targeted for low-income unorganised sector workers. These schemes help the unorganised sector workers, who do not have steady flow of regular income or low level of income, to save a small amount of their income during their working life. These accumulated funds then invested collectively through a pension fund managers (PFM) or PF house to generate returns. The total return is dependent on the accumulation of funds throughout the working life of the worker.

Post 2000, India witnessed the emergence of such schemes specially targeted for the low-income segment either through the Self-Help Groups (SHGs) or through the intermediary channel. For instance, Abhaya Hastham (AH), a co-contributory pension scheme for SHG members of Society for Eradication of Rural Poverty (SERP), an NGO promoted by the Andhra Pradesh state government, in 2009. Unit Trust of India (UTI), the asset management company, opened its Retirement Benefit Pension (UTI RBP) fund for low-income clients

Table 3.5 Old Age Pension Schemes in the States and Union Territories

State/ U.T.	Year of Introduction	Monthly Pension the time of Introduction of Scheme (Rs.)	Stipulated Age for Eligibility (Years)
Uttar Pradesh	1957	125	65
Andhra Pradesh	1960	75	65
Kerala	1960	110	65
Tamil Nadu	1962	150	65
Rajasthan	1964	200	58 (M) 55 (F)
West Bengal	1964	300	60
Karnataka	1965	100	65 (M) 60 (F)
Delhi	1968	200	60
Himachal Pradesh	1968	150	65
Punjab	1968	200	65 (M) 60 (F)
Haryana	1969	100	65
Chandigarh	1969	200	60
Bihar	1970	100	60
Madhya Pradesh	1970	150	60
Dadra Nagar Haveli	1974	75	60
Mizoram	1975	100	65 (M) 60 (F)
Orissa	1975	100	65
Lakshadweep	1975	100	60
Jammu & Kashmir	1976	125	55
Gujarat	1978	200	60
Tripura	1978	75	70
Nagaland	1979	100	70
Maharashtra	1980	100	65 (M) 60 (F)
Meghalaya	1980	75	65 (M) 60 (F)
Manipur	1981	75	65 (M) 60 (F)
Sikkim	1981	75	74 (M) 65 (F)
Andaman& Nicobar Islands	1981	75	60
Assam	1983	75	65 (M) 60 (F)
Goa	1983	75	60
Daman & Diu	1983	75	60
Pondicherry	1987	100	60
Arunachal Pradesh	1988	150	60

Source: Irudaya (2008), Kulkarni et al. (2018).
Note: Table prepared on chronological order of their implementation.

in 2006. Under the UTI-BRP, individuals invest regularly into funds and the accumulated funds are invested in a mix of equity and debt securities. A lot of NGOs and MFIs signed up to offer the product. But the first micro-pension was launched Self Employed Women Association (SEWA) in April 2006 and the immediate second micro pension scheme was launched by Bihar Milk Cooperative (COMFED) in September 2006.

Though micro pension schemes have some issues regarding the structuring of pay-out options and delivery mechanisms, researchers have pointed out that micro-pensions have the potential to be one of the most appropriate components in India's multi-tiered social security system and, therefore, these schemes should be promoted (Shankar and Asher, 2011).

3.4 Pension Reforms in India

The Ministry of Social Justice and Empowerment commissioned a project namely Old Age Social and Income Security (OASIS) under the chairmanship of Dr S. A. Dave to examine the policy related to old-age security in India in 1998. The eight-member expert committee submitted its report in 2000 and proposed a New Pension System (NPS) with DC system. Individuals are required to open an Individual Retirement Account (IRA) at the early stage of his/her life to start contributing to his/her own PF. The accumulated fund will be managed by the professional PFM to invest through "Safe Income", "Balance Income" and "Growth" style pension. The regulatory and development of the pension system would be entrusted into an independent and prudential regulator name Pension Fund Regulatory and Development Authority of India (PFRDA). The most developmental part of this pension scheme is the access to this Scheme with the help of Point of Presence (POP). Individuals would be able to access and operate their own pension account all over India from any POPs. These POPs could be Banks, Post Offices, depository participants or any other financial intermediaries located anywhere in India. NPS will have a centralised record keeping system of all the individual transactions through a centralised depository. With the available IT and communication system, the depositary would be able to provide a superior service at a low cost with less risk and fraud in the transactions (OASIS, 2000).

The fiscal burden of the DB pension system was the main factor driving the fundamental pension reforms for government employees (civil servants) by replacing DBs schemes and creating a system with individual DCs. The professionally managed PFM would manage the PFs with guidelines issued by the independent regulatory and development authority (Dave, 2006). Therefore, massive progress on the civil servants' pension is possible through careful, common-sense parametric reforms (Asher, 2000). The Union Cabinet approved the creation of an interim PFRDA by administrative order in August 2003,

Table 3.6 Number of Subscribers of Central Govt. and State Govt. Employees (in lakh) in NPS

S.N.	Sector	No. of Subscribers (in lakh)			Growth (%)
		31-Mar-19	31-Mar-20	31-Mar-21	YOY
A	CG	19.85	21.02	21.76	3.52
B	SG	43.21	47.54	51.41	8.13
C	**Sub Total (A+B)**	**63.06**	**68.56**	**73.17**	6.72

Source: Pension Bulletin, March 2021, PFRDA.

and decided to introduce National Pension System (NPS) [renaming the old New Pension System] for the Central Government employees joining on or after 1 January 2004 on a mandatory basis. Later NPS was extended to other government sectors such as autonomous bodies, state governments and union territories. By the end of March 2020, 29 states and union territories have introduced NPS for their employees (PFRDA, 2020; Table 3.6).

By the end of March 2021, there were 73.17 lakh (7.3 million) employees of central and state government employees are registered with the contributory NPS. Out of the total 73 lakh registered employees in NPS, states share is almost 70%. The NPS was also introduced to the other non-governmental formal sector such as corporates and registered organisations where formal employment is existing. There are 11.25 lakh (1.12 million) employees/workers from the corporate sector is registered with this new contributory pension system, NPS by the end of March 2021. The total coverage mentioned above is all in the organised sector where formal employment is provided apart from the beneficiaries associated with EPFO.

3.4.1 *Progress of NPS in India*

Since inception the growth in the total number of subscribers in various schemes under the NPS was modest as it grew from 0.4 million subscribers in 2009 to 8.75 million subscribers in 2015. After 2016, the growth in the NPS schemes is very encouraging. The number of subscribers has increased by 22.8% from 34.56 million in March 2020 to 42.44 million in March 2021 (Table 3.7). Therefore, the respective contribution to the NPS has also increased by 29.66% from Rs. 3,252.19 billion in March 2020 to Rs. 4,216.77 billion in March 2021 (Table 3.8).

Table 3.7 Total Number of Subscribers in NPS (in lakh)

S.N.	Sector	No. of Subscribers (in million)			Growth (%)	% Share
		31-Mar-19	*31-Mar-20*	*31-Mar-21*	*YOY*	
A	CG	1.98	2.10	2.17	3.51	5
B	SG	4.32	4.75	5.14	8.13	12
C	**Sub Total (A+B)**	**6.30**	**6.85**	**7.31**		**17**
D	Corporate	0.80	0.97	1.12	15.64	3
E	All Citizen	0.93	1.25	1.64	31.53	4
F	**Sub Total (D+E)**	**1.73**	**2.22**	**2.76**		**7**
G	NPS Lite	4.36	4.33	4.30	−0.69	10
H	APY	14.95	21.14	28.04	32.67	66
I	**Grand Total (C+F+G+H)**	**27.35**	**34.55**	**42.44**	**22.82**	**100**

Source: Annual Pension Bulletin-2021, PFRDA.

Table 3.8 Total Contribution in NPS (Rs. In Crore)

S.N.	Sector	Contribution (Rs. In Crore)			Growth (%)	% Share
		31-Mar-19	*31-Mar-20*	*31-Mar-21*	*YOY*	
A	CG	78,379	99,740	123,124	23.44	29
B	SG	124,191	165,190	214,710	29.98	51
C	**Sub Total (A+B)**	**202,570**	**264,930**	**337,834**		**80**
D	Corporate	24,437	32,829	44,711	36.19	11
E	All Citizen	9,685	15,012	22,510	49.95	5
F	**Sub Total (D+E)**	**34,122**	**47,841**	**67,221**		**16**
G	NPS Lite	2,555	2,701	2,858	5.83	1
H	APY	6,335	9,747	13,764	41.21	3
I	**Grand Total (C+F+G+H)**	**245,582**	**3,25,219**	**4,21,677**	**29.66**	**100**

Source: Annual Pension Bulletin-2021, PFRDA.

3.4.2 Performance of NPS Funds in India

The contribution made by the subscribers are managed and invested by the PFs, an intermediary, which are registered with the Pension Fund Regulatory and Development Authority (PFRDA). PFs for Government Sector NPS Schemes (i.e. CG and SG), NPS Lite and APY are managed by the three PFs:

  i   LIC Pension Fund Limited,
 ii   SBI Pension Funds Private Ltd and
iii   UTI Retirement Solutions Ltd.

The Private Sector NPS schemes are managed by the following PF:

  i   HDFC Pension Management Co. Ltd,
 ii   ICICI Prudential Pension Fund Management Co. Ltd,
iii   Kotak Mahindra Pension Fund Ltd,
 iv   LIC Pension Fund Ltd,
  v   SBI Pension Funds Pvt. Ltd,
 vi   UTI Retirement Solutions Pvt. Ltd and
vii   Birla Sun Life Pension Management Limited.

The investment management fee charged by PFs for managing the Government Sector schemes and Private Sector schemes is 0.0102% and is 0.01% per annum of the Assets under Management (AUM). The AUM of the PFs have also increased many folds from Rs. 23 billion in 2009 to little more than Rs. 5,780 billion in 2021. The AUM has grown by 38.46% during the financial year 2022–21 despite the impact of Covid-19 on the economy (Table 3.9).

PFs were performing robustly and their returns are comparable with the benchmark return which is the composite performance of government securities (G-secs), corporate bonds, equities and money market instruments, aggregated in the ratio of 49%, 35%, 14% and 2%, respectively. The schemes wise PF performance since inception is provided in Table 3.10.

3.4.3 NPS and EPF

The NPS and the Employees' Provident Fund (EPF) are the two most common pension schemes that provide old-age security. Both the schemes offer investment alternatives for employees along with tax-saving benefits.

Table 3.9 Total Assets under Management (AUM) in NPS (Rs. in Crore)

S.N.	Sector	AUM (Rs. In Crore)			Growth (%)	% Share
		Mar-19	31-Mar-20	Mar-21	YOY	
A	CG	109,010	138,046	181,788	31.69	31
B	SG	158,491	211,023	291,381	38.08	50
C	Sub Total (A+B)	267,501	349,069	473,169		82
D	Corporate	30,875	41,243	62,609	51.80	11
E	All Citizen	9,569	12,913	22,206	71.96	4
F	Sub Total (D+E)	40,444	54,156	84,815		15
G	NPS Lite	3,409	3,728	4,354	16.80	1
H	APY	6,860	10,526	15,687	49.03	3
I	Grand Total (C+F+G+H)	3,18,214	4,17,479	5,78,025	38.46	100

Source: Annual Pension Bulletin-2021, PFRDA.

Table 3.10 NPS Returns since Inception (in %)

Pension Funds→		SBI	LIC	UTI	ICICI	KOTAK	HDFC	BIRLA
CG		10.11	9.86	9.85				
SG		9.80	9.86	9.85				
Corporate-CG		10.00	10.05					
TIER I	A	9.43	7.78	5.81	6.79	7.43	8.26	5.84
	E	10.28	12.09	11.78	11.90	11.14	14.81	12.18
	C	10.51	10.26	9.43	10.46	10.10	10.47	9.98
	G	9.86	11.28	8.85	9.12	9.08	10.28	9.15
'	E	10.08	9.62	10.47	10.26	10.49	12.63	12.09
TIER II	C	10.09	9.60	9.50	10.32	9.38	9.56	8.93
	G	9.88	11.54	9.57	9.23	8.85	10.45	8.04
NPS Swavalamban		10.37	10.39	10.34		10.19		
APY		9.55	9.89	9.97				

Source: Annual Pension Bulletin-2021, PFRDA.

The returns offered by the EPF are fixed and the rate of interest is announced by the Finance Ministry, Government of India, annually. However, the return on NPS is dependent on the investment choices made by the subscribers of a particular scheme and the return may rise or fall. Therefore, EPF offers assured returns and security, while NPS offers higher returns with element of risk associated with the investments outcome. Thus, for the common man both options offer tax advantages and good returns (Figure 3.3).

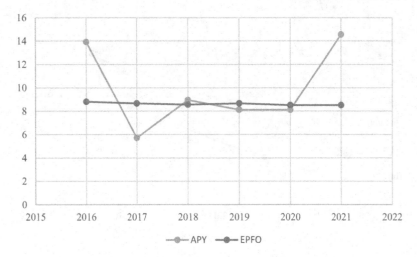

Figure 3.3 Return of EPF and APY.
Source: Annual Reports, EPFO & PFRDA (2015–21).

Since the NPS started recently, the number of total subscribers are less than the EPF. But the AUM with the NPS is improving very steadily and very close to the EPF. By the end of the financial year 2020–21, the AUM of NPS and EPFO are Rs. 5,780,240 million and Rs. 5,935,465 million, respectively (Figure 3.4).

All the employees covered under the EPF scheme now have the option to switch to NPS scheme and can avail all the tax benefits and savings that are applicable under NPS. The choice between NPS and EPF depends on the financial knowledge of the employee, risk appetite, returns, security, liquidity, maturity, etc. (Figure 3.5).

3.5 Schemes for the Unorganised Sector

Institutionalised social security schemes in an organised manner for workers in the unorganised sector to protect and provide old-age security were not available just after the independence in India. The first organised system of inclusive pension scheme initiative was the creation of **Public Provident Fund (PPF)** in June 1968 to promote small savings and investments by the National Savings Organization (NSO). This PPF scheme is a long-term savings instrument similar to those contributory schemes available to the organised/formal sector employees. Therefore, this is the first scheme that was envisioned at

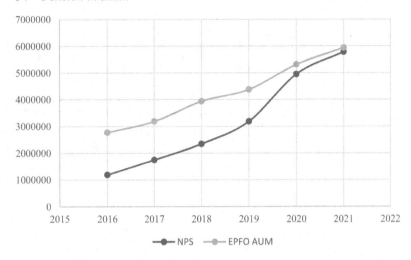

Figure 3.4 AUM under NPS and EPFO since 2016.
Source: Annual Reports, EPFO & PFRDA (2015–21).

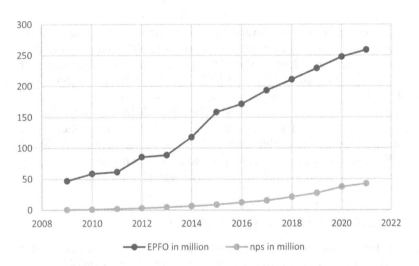

Figure 3.5 Comparison of EPFO and NPS Subscriber since 2009.
Source: Annual Reports, EPFO & PFRDA (2015–20).

getting unorganised sector workers to contribute towards their old-age pension requirements.

This scheme was offered initially through public sector banks and later post offices were also included in 1979[1] to reach more rural areas and to include more people. The scheme has an investment limit with minimum of Rs. 100 (fixed in 1968) and a maximum of Rs. 60,000 per annum for 15 years maturity. Thereafter, the term can be extended in incremental blocks of five years. The rate of interest is determined by central govt. on a quarterly basis. The interest rate was fixed at 12% when the scheme introduced and the Government of India had to pay a fixed interest-bearing of 12% on the accumulated corpus of the individual.

Despite the fact that the scheme's focus was to include more and more unorganised people/workers into the contributory savings with higher interest rates than the market, the scheme failed to attract more people into the ambit of this PPF scheme. After three decades of the rolling out of this scheme, the coverage was only 1% of the total working population by the end of 1999 (OASIS, 2000).

The contribution limit has increased a minimum of Rs. 500 to a maximum of Rs. 100,000 per annum at present and the interest rate on PPF is 7.10% per annum[2] with effect from 01.04.2020. PPF didn't deliver its basic objective to cover and protect the unorganised sector during their old age and has become a tax saving investment scheme, due to its tax exemption, for the lower- and middle-income group of people. It has been found that during the last 16 years, (from financial year 2002–03 to 2018–19) the number of individuals who filed tax return increased to 66% but the actual tax payers have increased only by 22% which confirms the use of tax savings investment methods (such as PPF) being used to pay less or no tax (Table 3.11).[3]

Along with PPF, there was the emergence of different **worker-welfare boards** at the individual state level for the diverse occupational groups, such as construction workers, auto workers, beedi workers, handloom workers, porter, etc. The state legislatures have enacted an Act solely focusing on the welfare of the workers, known as the Labour Welfare Fund Act, in the areas of health care service, infant welfare, education, housing, marriage, etc. Therefore, the fund is a statutory body which determines the contribution amount and frequency of the contribution of the state and individual worker into the fund. The contribution amount of state and individual workers along with the periodicity of payment differs from state to state. Some state governments pay annually, some half-yearly and some states labour welfare funds may pay monthly contributions to the respective funds.

Table 3.11 Labour Welfare Fund – (State Wise) 2020 in India

S No	State	Employee Contribution	Employer Contribution	Total	Period	Due Date	Last Date
1	Andhra Pradesh	30	70	100	Yearly		December 31 January 31
2	Chhattisgarh	15	45	60	Half yearly	June	30 December 31 July 15 January 15
3	Chandigarh	2	4	6	Monthly	Last Date of Month	April 15 October 15
4	Delhi	0.75	2.25	3	Half yearly	June 30	December 31 July 15 January 15
5	Goa	60	180	240	Half yearly		June 30 December 31 July 15 January 15
6	Gujarat	6	12	318	Half yearly		June 30 December 31 July 15 January 15
7	Haryana	10	20	30	Monthly	Every month	Last date of Month
8	Karnataka	20	40	60	Yearly		December 31 January 31
9	Kerala	20	20	40	Monthly	Every month	Fifth of every month
10	Madhya Pradesh	10	30	40	Half yearly		June 30 December 31 July 15 January 15

11	Maharashtra				Half yearly	June 30 December 31	July 15 January 15
	Wages up to 3000	6	18	24			
	Wages above 3000	12	36	48			
12	Odisha	20	40	60	Half yearly	June 30 December 31	July 15 January 15
13	Punjab	5	20	25	Monthly	Every month	April 15 October 15
14	Tamil Nadu	10	20	30	Yearly	December 31	January 31
15	Telangana	2	5	7	Yearly	December 31	January 31
16	West Bengal	13	6	9	Half yearly	June 30 December 31	July 15 January 15

Source: Compiled from Rajesh (2021). Available at: https://www.hrcabin.com/labour-welfare-fund-state-wise-in-india/

These old-age social security (pension) schemes are available to a wide range of unorganised sector workers, including semi-formal or informal workers such as agricultural labourers, handloom workers, auto-rickshaw drivers, salt workers, tailors and barbers. Approximately 8.85 million people were covered by these schemes by the end of 2006. The maximum number of workers in the unorganised sector are protected with the pension schemes of these welfare boards in India (Asher, 2007).

3.5.1 Problems with the Schemes

Even with attractive benefits and generous government contributions, many of these welfare board schemes have not accomplished the intended coverage in the long term. For example, out of the total construction workers of 5.3 crores only 3.8 crores are registered with Construction welfare Boards.[4] Many of the schemes are based on DB system, which has become unsustainable due to payment obligations. All the funds are guided by the government rules which prohibit the funds to invest in other investment sources apart from govt. securities and eventually earning low returns making the fund unsustainable or unprofitable for the beneficiaries in the long run. It is also found that the funds are not managed professionally and a huge corpus is sitting idle to be utilised efficiently.[5] Recently, the Comptroller and Auditor General of India (CAG) has filed an affidavit in the Delhi High Court that there are instances of "irregular expenditure" of funds accumulated with the Delhi Building and Other Construction Workers (DBOCW) Welfare Board. In the report CAG opined that *"The board may increase its efforts to provide more welfare measures to the construction workers so that the amount of cess collected is utilised for the purpose for which it is collected"*[6]

Similarly, in the case of EPFO, the fund is managed poorly and the EPF pay-outs have surpassed returns from the investments in medium and long-term government securities. The mandated investment guideline stops EPFO to invest other than government securities. This means that the EPFO is paying out more than it earns from investments. This gap has widened significantly since 2000–01, making it unsustainable for the long term unless some reforms are incorporated in EPFO in managing its investment and running the organisation more effectively (Asher, 2007). Though there is a proposal to hand over control of the EPFO corpus of over Rs. 10 lakh crores (INR 10 trillion) under the PF, pension and insurance schemes to a central body.[7]

3.5.2 Other Schemes

In addition to the above schemes, Government of India launched the "Unorganised Sector Workers" Social Security Scheme, in January 2004 on pilot basis in 50 districts covering all the states on a contributory basis to provide old-age pension of Rs. 500/- per month on attaining the age of 60 years. The worker needs to contribute Rs. 50 per month (18–35 years) and Rs. 100 per month (36–50 years). The employer was required to contribute Rs. 100 per month with the Government's contribution of 1.16% of the workers' wages as available in the organised sector. The scheme was under the EPFO and it is found that the scheme was unsustainable since it has no statutory support and was voluntary in nature. The scheme later scarped as it was not financially viable (Planning Commission, 2006).

Other than the Governmental efforts, numerous public institutions and several agencies are also providing different kinds of social security benefits to selected groups of workers in the unorganised sector, such as Self-Employed Women's Association (SEWA, The Working Women's Forum India (WWF), and the Mathadi Workers Boards (MWB), Co-operative Development Foundation (CDF), SAMAKHYA, Trivandrum District Fishermen Federation (TDFF), the Association of Sarwa Sewa Farms (ASSF), the Society for Promotion of Area Resources Centre (SPARC), Voluntary Health Services (VHS), etc. (Planning Commission, 2001).

Apart from the schemes discussed above, some privately managed contributory pension schemes are available in India for low-income people. For example, the asset management company UTI opened a scheme named UTI's Retirement Benefit Pension (UTI RBP fund for low-income groups of people in 2006. Under this scheme, individuals regularly contribute into their personal account and the payments are invested in UTI RBP fund which invests in the market. Pension is allowed at the age of 58 and accumulated funds can be withdrawn earlier with an exit charge.

3.6 National Pension System (NPS) for Unorganised Sector

For the reason that the schemes which were specifically designed for the unorganised sector like, PPF/welfare funds or schemes like EPF are mismanaged and become unsustainable to extend coverage to the unorganised sector. Therefore, voluntary retirement savings or contributory pension schemes for old-age security have emerged as an alternative and important policy tool to spread out the coverage of pension facilities in India.

The new contributory pension scheme, NPS, is a professionally managed low cost, high return and financially viable pension product. To improve the higher pension coverage of the unorganised sector workers and encourage people from the unorganised sector to voluntarily save for their old-age security, the Government launched the co-contribution scheme – NPS-Lite/Swavlamban scheme in September 2010 as an important policy measure.

NPS-Lite schemes are basically designed to protect the future of the economically disadvantaged people and who are not financially sound. To encourage the contribution, the Government also contributed Rs. 1,000 per year with the similar contribution for the age group of 18–60 years. Despite its various attractive features, NPS-Lite succeeded in attracting only 43.02 lakh registered subscribers over the last few years (PFRDA, 2021). The failure of the NPS-Lite pension schemes was credited to its structure also. In this scheme, pension Aggregators are being paid a commission of Rs. 100 per client, but subscribers also need to maintain the minimum contribution of Rs. 1,000 per year. Thus, most Aggregator firms focused only on financially strong workers or a steady stream of income. This approach inevitably excluded a big section of low-income unorganised sector workers, who otherwise would have made petite or small contributions to maintain and retain the membership in NPS-Lite (Palacios and Sane, 2013). This was also found that most unorganised sector workers are financially not literate and lack investment decisions. Since the investments in this scheme is for the long term, and the return is based on the investments, it was difficult to provide a guaranteed pension. The lack of awareness among the unorganised sector workers and ineffective communication about the scheme from the Government is also one reason for this scheme's failure (Rajsekhar et al., 2016).

NPS-Lite was discontinued in 2015 and the fresh enrolments under NPS-Lite Scheme had been discontinued w.e.f 01.04.2015. Subsequently, a new revived guaranteed pension scheme, Atal Pension Yojana (APY) was launched on 9 May 2015 by the Prime Minister of India.

The Scheme, **Atal Pension Yojana (APY)** is open to all citizens of India with a bank account in the age group of 18–40 years, but it is specifically targeted to the unorganised sector workers to encourage them for contributory regular small savings and provide a pension to protect them in their old age. Under the Atal Pension Yojana (APY), the subscribers would receive Government guaranteed fixed minimum pension of Rs. 1,000 per month, Rs. 2,000 per month, Rs. 3,000 per month, Rs. 4,000 per month and Rs. 5,000 per month, at the age of 60 years, depending on their contributions at various levels of entry ages. There is an improvement from the NPS-Lite schemes, and all the shortcomings are covered with this Scheme. Table 3.12 presents the fundamental differences of both schemes.

With the introduction of the APY, it was expected that more people from the unorganised sector would join this scheme due to Government guaranteed minimum pension benefit. But during the last five years, the scheme could attract only 2.54 crores people (Table 3.13), which was way beyond policy makers' expectations. Only in the last financial year there was a growth of 27% in the total number of subscribers which is probably because people have faced the hardship during Covid-19 crisis and were more concerned about their future source of income. The return of these schemes is quite steady and fund managers have given a return of more than 9.5% in APY and more than 10% in NPS-Lite (Table 3.14).

3.7 Other Contributory Schemes for Unorganised Sector

The Government of India has introduced two[8] voluntary and contributory pension schemes specifically targeting the unorganised sector workers in February 2019[9];

1 **Pradhan Mantri Shram Yogi Maan-dhan Yojana, (PM-SYM)** and
2 **National Pension Scheme for the Traders and Self-Employed Persons Yojana.**

3.7.1 Pradhan Mantri Shram Yogi Maan-dhan Yojana (PM-SYM)

PM-SAY is an old-age security scheme or a pension scheme specially designed for the unorganised sector workers who are engaged in as rickshaw pullers, street vendors, mid-day meal workers, head loaders, brick kiln workers, cobblers, rag pickers, domestic workers, washer men, home-based workers, own account workers, agricultural workers, construction workers, beedi workers, handloom workers, leather workers or in similar other occupations with a minimum assured pension of Rs. 3,000 per month after attaining the age of 60 years. This Scheme is attractive to the workers because central Government would also contribute the equal amount based on their age of joining the Scheme (Table 3.15). Anyone who are having a bank account and

Table 3.12 A Comparison between NPS-Lite and APY

Feature	NPS-Lite	APY
Joining age	Under 60 years of age at the time of joining	Between 18 and 40 years at the time of joining.
Minimum contribution	Rs. 100 at the time of registration. No minimum Prescribed amount in subsequent years.	Fixed amount depends on age of joining/ minimum pension desired
Pension amount	Depends on subscriber contributions and investment return.	Minimum guaranteed amount Rs. 1,000/2,000/3,000/ 4,000/5,000
Penalty for payment delay	None	Up to Rs. 10 per month for overdue payment
Penalty for payment default	None	APY account frozen/ deactivated/closed after 6/12/24 months of continuous non-payment
Government co-contribution	Rs. 1,000 per year for contributions between Rs. 1,000 and Rs. 12,000 per year	Fifty percent of contribution or up to Rs. 1,000 per annum (whichever is low)
Co-contribution period	Till 2016–17	Till 2019–20.(enrolled before March 31, 2016)
Agency incentive	Rs. 120 for new enrolments and Rs. 100 for Persistent Subscriptions who contribute at least Rs. 1,000 per year	Volume –based incentive of up to Rs. 150 for new enrolments to banks
Bank account requirement	None	Yes. (Banks or Post office)
Contribution mode	Physical payment	Auto-debit from saving account
Customer service interface	Aggregator and CRA	Bank and CRA
Exit criterion	Yes, Before 60 years. Subscribers between 18 and 40 years of age are eligible to migrate to APY	Voluntary exit before 60 years. No Govt. contribution in case of r voluntary exit before 60 years.

Source: FAQ, APY (PFRDA). Available at: https://www.pfrda.org.in/myauth/admin/showimg.cshtml?ID=1789

Table 3.13 Number of Subscribers of NPS Lite and APY

S.N.	Sector	No. of Subscribers (in lakh)			Growth (%)
		31-Mar-19	31-Mar-20	31-Mar-21	YOY
A	NPS Lite	43.63	43.32	43.02	−0.69
B	APY	149.53	211.42	280.49	32.67
C	**Sub Total (A+B)**	**193.16**	**254.74**	**323.51**	**26.99**

Source: Pension Bulletin, March 2021, PFRDA.

Table 3.14 Returns on NPS-Lite/APY since Inception (in %) (as on 31st March, 2021)

Pension Funds	SBI	LIC	UTI
NPS-Lite/Swavalamban	10.37%	10.39%	10.34%
APY	9.55%	9.89%	9.97%

Source: Pension Bulletin, March 2021, PFRDA.

Aadhar card, aged between 18 and 40 years are eligible for the PM-SAY provided his/her income is less than Rs. 15,000. PM-SYM Scheme will be administered by the Ministry of Labour and Employment (MoLE) and implemented through Life Insurance Corporation of India (LICI and CSC e-Governance Services India Limited and the fund of this Scheme will be under the responsibility of LICI as the Fund Manager. Once the worker joins the PM-SAY, the monthly contribution to the Scheme and the monthly pay out of pension, after attaining the super-annuation age of 60, would be carried out automatically through the Direct Benefit Transfer (DBT) system. The schemes have the flexibility in early withdrawal and exit. Family pension is applicable to the PM-SAY, i.e., after his/ her death, spouse will receive a monthly family pension which is 50% of the pension.[10] By the end of March 2021, little more than 44.94 lakh (4.4 million) unorganised sector workers have joined the Scheme.[11]

3.7.2 National Pension Scheme for the Traders and Self-Employed Persons Yojana

National Pension Scheme for Traders and Self-Employed Persons Yojana is a voluntary and contributory Government Pension Scheme for old age protection and social security of Vyaparis for a

Table 3.15 Contribution by the Worker and Central Govt. in PM-SAY

Entry Age	Superannuation Age	Member's Monthly Contribution (Rs)	Central Govt.'s Monthly Contribution (Rs)	Total Monthly Contribution (Rs)
(1)	(2)	(3)	(4)	(5) = (3) + (4)
18	60	55	55	110
19	60	58	58	116
20	60	61	61	122
21	60	64	64	128
22	60	68	68	136
23	60	72	72	144
24	60	76	76	152
25	60	80	80	160
26	60	85	85	170
27	60	90	90	180
28	60	95	95	190
29	60	100	100	200
30	60	105	105	210
31	60	110	110	220
32	60	120	120	240
33	60	130	130	260
34	60	140	140	280
35	60	150	150	300
36	60	160	160	320
37	60	170	170	340
38	60	180	180	360
39	60	190	190	380
40	60	200	200	400

Source: Ministry of Labour and Employment; Govt. of India. (https://labour.gov.in/brief-pm-sym)

minimum assured monthly pension of Rs. 3,000 after attaining the age of 60 years. These retail traders/petty shopkeepers and/or self-employed persons are typically working as retail traders, rice mill owners, oil mill owners, shop owners, workshop owners, commission agents, brokers of real estate, owners of small hotels, restaurants and other Vyaparis. To be eligible for the scheme the entry age limit is 18–40 years and retail traders with annual turn-over not exceeding Rs. 1.5 crore. They should not also be an income tax payer or a subscriber of any National Pension Scheme (NPS), Employees' State Insurance Corporation scheme (ESIC) and Employees' Provident Fund Organization (EPFO) and Pradhan Mantri Shram Yogi Maandhan. After the death of the subscriber his/her spouse will receive a monthly family pension which is equivalent to 50%

of the subscriber pension. The National Pension Scheme for Traders and Self Employed Persons Yojana is implemented by MoL&E, Government of India. In this scheme, similar to the PM-SAY, the central Government would also contribute an equal amount based on their age of joining the scheme (same as Table 3.9). Just like other schemes, in this case also, the potential subscriber should have a bank account and Aadhar card to make the contribution and pay out pensions through DBT.[12]

The National Pension Scheme for Traders and Self-Employed Persons has failed to attract an adequate number of subscribers as only about 25,000 persons have opted for the Scheme by the end of January 2020.[13]

3.8 Existing Pension Coverage in India

The total number of people employed in the organised sector, which includes central Government, state government, quasi-government bodies, local bodies and organised private sector, is 3 crores (CMIE, 2021) people under formal pension cover. The total unorganised sector people covered through NPS (NPS-Lite & APY) is 3.23 crores (Table 3.7). Therefore, the total working population under any pension cover is 6.23 crores (3 crores of unorganised sector and 3.23 crores from unorganised sector).

The total working population of India, at present, is estimated to be 45 crores (or 450 million). Out of this total workforce, 93%, i.e. about 41.85 crores, of people working in the unorganised sector of the country (Economic Survey 2018–19). Therefore, the total coverage of old-age security or pension to the whole workforce of India is only 13.84% of the working population. Overall, almost 86% working population in India doesn't have any pension coverage by the end of March 2021. This coverage is way behind the average people covered under any pension system of many countries. Approximately 96.8 crores (or 968 million) people were covered by the two basic public pension insurance systems in China by 2019. Around 435 million of them were covered by the public pension insurance for urban employees, the rest were covered by the public insurance for urban-rural residents.[14]

The merit of existing pension systems available to all segments of workers varies greatly across the countries. The Global Pension Index 2019,[15] based on the weights of adequacy, sustainability and integrity of the schemes, compares 37 pension systems throughout the World and finds that the Netherlands and Denmark have the best pension system in the World and graded them as "A" which is a first class and robust retirement system that delivers good benefits with high integrity and sustainable in nature. The index graded the Indian pension system as "D" (along with Japan, China, Mexico, the Philippines, Turkey, Argentina and Thailand) which means a pension system that has some desirable features but also has weaknesses that need to be addressed (MCGPI, 2020).

The voluntary and contributory pension coverage among the unorganised sector workers in India is merely, 7.72% (3.23 crores out of total estimated 41.85 crores unorganised sector workers). Therefore, 92.2% of workers engaged in an unorganised sector in India are out of old-age social security. This shows that the workers, labourers or any other working population in the informal sectors of the economy are forced to work after the age of 60 years to sustain life after the retirement stage or they are dependent on other sources of income such as saving, investment, inherited property/land, dependent on their children. It is found that 33% of the elderly are economically vulnerable, and half of the elderly are financially dependent on others (60% in West Bengal and Tamil Nadu). Almost 25% of the elderly in India do not possess any assets (UNFPA, 2012a).

The central and state government employees are the major subscribers of NPS, which was specially meant for the unorganised sector. Thus, NPS has not served its prime objective of covering the most uncovered sector, the unorganised sector in India. This is essential for the policymakers to know, why such low enrolment in the contributory pension schemes in India. Therefore, it is important for policymakers to study the financial behaviour of unorganised sector workers in India to explore more into the subject of non-participation in contributory pension schemes.

3.9 India's Demographic Transition

India is witnessing a demographic change into an increasing number of aged persons. Policymakers should note this transition in their possible policy reforms to pension benefits or old-age security system or any other welfare programmes. Population ageing is expected to impact the individual earnings and their consumption vis-à-vis savings behaviour. According to the UN Populations projections 2019 database, India's projected population (medium variant) after 30 years (or in 2050) would be as high as 1.63 billion or 163 crores (Figure 3.6).

With the improved standard of living and betterment of health sciences for the mankind, the life expectancy at birth has improved

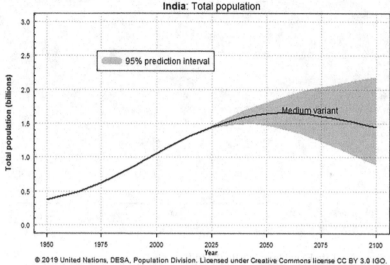

Figure 3.6 Population's Projections: India.

ever before and it is expected to improve from the present level of 69.9 years (2020) to 75 years in 2050 (Figure 3.7) in India. If we look at the projection of life expectancy of elderly in India, we can see that life expectancy of elderly in India is expected to increase at every stage. At the age of 60 years, the life expectancy would go to 20 years in 2050 from the present level of 18.34 years. Similarly, at the age of 70 years, it is expected to increase from 11.77 years in 2020 to almost 13 years at the end of 2050 (Table 3.16). This means that the elderly people in India are going to live more which would expose them to the longevity risk.[16] An imperative consequence of longer life or higher life expectancy increases the healthcare expenditure. The Out-of-Pocket-Expenditure (OOPE)[17] in health by the household is one of the highest (71%) in the World in India.[18] Typical individual expenses increase disproportionately with age and, therefore, elderly would be in need of more support at their old age.

The share of elderly population out of the total population is also increasing day by day. India is not an exception either. The total population above 65 years old is projected at 225.4 million; that is 22.5 crores from the present level of 9 crores only, which is 13.75% of total population of India in 2050 (Figure 3.8). The UN Population Division estimates that in India, there will be 21.16% of the population above

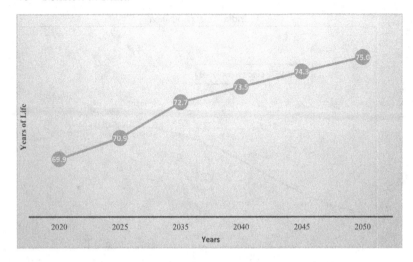

Figure 3.7 Life Expectancy at Birth (India).
Source: UN, DESA, Population Division. https://population.un.org/wpp/.

Table 3.16 Projected Life Expectancy of Elderly in India (at Different Age
        Levels)

Age	2020–25	2025–30	2030–35	2035–40	2040–45	2045–50
At 60 Years	18.34	18.66	19	19.34	19.7	20.07
At 70 Years	11.77	11.99	12.22	12.46	12.71	12.98
At 80 Years	6.95	7.06	7.18	7.3	7.43	7.58

Source: UN, DESA, Population Division. https://population.un.org/wpp/.

the age of 60 years in 2050 as compared to 60.34% aged between 15 and
59 years in 2020 (Figure 3.9).

The structure of the demography is going to change from 2020 to
2030. The population pyramids of 2020 and for 2050 (Figures 3.10 and
3.11) explain the transition of Indian demography. New demographic
change would also have growing impact on the old-age dependency
ratio[19] in India as we can see an expected increase in the same from 9.8
in 2020 to 20.3 dependents in 2050 (Figure 3.9).

The ability of developing countries, such as India, to deal effectively
with the social and economic impact of ageing populations is very
much restricted by their low levels of economic conditions and poor
human capital (Ingham et al., 2009). The old-age participation rate

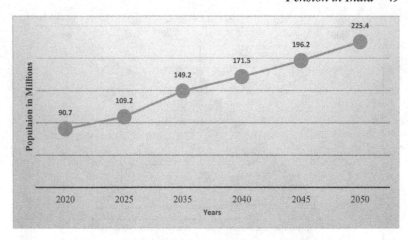

Figure 3.8 Projection of Population above 65 Years Old.
Source: UN, DESA, Population Division. https://population.un.org/wpp/.

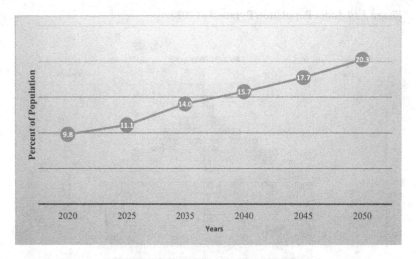

Figure 3.9 Old-Age Dependency Ratio Projection.
Source: UN, DESA, Population Division. https://population.un.org/wpp/.

in India is also one of the lowest in the world. The old-age workers in India are not skilled enough to participate again in the workforce. On the other hand, the and this makes the Fiscal burden on the generous non-contributory (DB) public pension schemes for central and state government employees with increasing number of beneficiaries

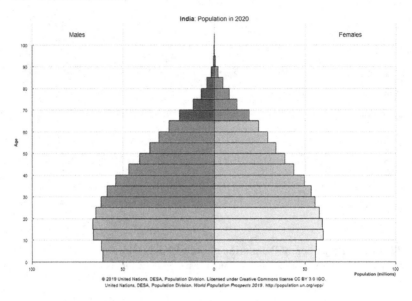

Figure 3.10 India Population Pyramid at 2020.

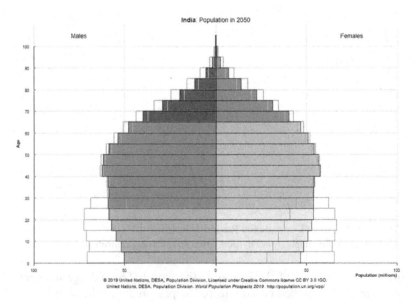

Figure 3.11 India Population Pyramid at 2050.

making it financially unsustainable in near future unless the current pension system is adjusted (Asher, 2000).

Civil servants (state and central) in India are only about 3% of the total labour force but their retirement benefits are almost equivalent to 2% of GDP (Asher, 2007). The combined budget for pension and other retirement benefits surged from Rs. 165,958 crores in 2010–2–11 to Rs. 413,435 crores in 2017–18 (MoF, 2019).

The increase in number of aged, traditional and informal methods for old-age security, such as joint family system, big families or having a male child for their support in the old age in India, are gradually unable to cope with increasing life span and upsurge in medical cost age. Therefore, there is a mounting stress in the low-income group of people and more so in the old age. Since the enrolment in the NPS has been poor and has only covered 7.7% of unorganised sector workers in India, it is crucial for the policymakers to know why such low enrolment in contributory pension schemes in India. Therefore, this work would evaluate the awareness level about the NPS and financial behaviour of unorganised sector workers in India.

Notes

1 Govt. of India, MoF, (DEA) Notification no. GSR 1136 dated 15.06.1968 and further amended time to time. [Available at: http://www.nsiindia.gov.in/InternalPage.aspx?Id_Pk=79].
2 "Revision of interest rates for Small Savings Schemes for first quarter of Financial Year 2020–21" (PDF). dea.gov.in/. March 31 2020. Retrieved March 31 2020.
3 https://economictimes.indiatimes.com/wealth/tax/budget-2020-the-deceptive-rise-in-indias-income-tax-base/articleshow/73868046.cms?from=mdr
4 https://pib.gov.in/PressReleasePage.aspx?PRID=1607911 (on 24 MAR 2020)
5 https://timesofindia.indiatimes.com/city/bengaluru/rs-7500-crore-welfare-fund-underused-in-karnataka/articleshow/83358906.cms
6 https://realty.economictimes.indiatimes.com/news/regulatory/-construction-workers-welfare-cess-fund-accumulated-with-board-cag-to-hc/76958164
7 https://economictimes.indiatimes.com/news/economy/policy/govt-proposes-to-corporatise-epfo-esic-appointment-of-ceos-for-first-time/articleshow/71188466.cms
8 Another similar old-age pension scheme introduced by the Government for all land holding (up to 2 hectares) Small and Marginal Farmers (SMFs) in the country as Pradhan Mantri Kisan Maandhan.
9 https://labour.gov.in/sites/default/files/Budget_Speech.pdf
10 https://maandhan.in/page/faq
11 https://labour.gov.in/dashboard

12 https://maandhan.in/scheme/pmvmy
13 https://economictimes.indiatimes.com/news/economy/finance/national-pension-scheme-for-traders-fails-to-gain-traction/articleshow/73107667.cms.
14 https://www.statista.com/statistics/234072/number-of-pension-insurance-contributors-in-china/
15 Melbourne Mercer Global Pension Index 2019.
16 Longevity Risk: The risk that resources may not be adequate throughout life-time of an individual.
17 Out-of-pocket payments are spending on health directly out-of-pocket by households.
18 https://data.worldbank.org/indicator/SH.XPD.OOPC.CH.ZS?locations=IN
19 The ratio of older dependents – people older than 64 – to the working-age population – those aged 15–64. Data are shown as the proportion of dependents per 100 working-age population (UN, DESA).

4 Research and Development in Pension Financial Literacy

4.1 Review of the Status of Research and Development in the Subject

With the time financial markets have been producing and offering many products which are very complex and even hard for financially sound investors in the market. Therefore, it has become very difficult for common people to understand those products and take their own financial decision. Pension products are also very complex and deal with long-term investments which are very difficult for normal people to evaluate and take investments decision as they lack knowledge in the case of numeracy, inflation and time value of money. A lot of studies have been conducted to understand the financial literacy of different groups or subgroups of people in the world. We will make our discussion limited to unorganised sector, their status and financial literacy in pension products.

4.2 Unorganised Sector and Poverty and Social Security

Expressing the concern for the weak informal sector in the developing countries, Canagarajah and Sethuraman (2001) find that the workers in this sector constitute a significant part of the employed population without any cover of social security in India. If this major proportion of the sector is taken into consideration, then their contribution to the Gross Domestic Product is also noteworthy in many developing countries (Blunch et al., 2001). The informal sector accounts for about 28% of the GDP, while in India, 32.4% of the GDP is contributed by the informal sector, which is worth considerable (Charmes, 1999a). According to Canagarajah and Sethuraman (2001), the informal sector accounted for 77% of the net domestic product, and it is not under any social security cover. Recent statistics show that the share of formal/informal sectors across broad sectors to GVA (in %) is little more than 52% in India (Murhty, 2019).

Ninety-three percent of the total workforce is working in the informal/unorganised sector, contributing almost half of the total GDP. Due to the higher proportion of participation of workers in the unorganised/informal sector, a considerable portion of its workers are more inclined towards poverty, for example, the study by Sethuraman (1997) finds that most of the Latin American poor workers belong to the informal sector and the similar trend was found in other countries such as 66.4% in Brazil, 66.2% in Bolivia, as high as 87.1% in Panama. The relative frequency of poverty is found very high in the informal sector. In India also the situation is not much different than the other countries mentioned above. Approximately 93% of casual workers do not have any written job contract in India (MoLE, 2015), making them vulnerable and forcing them to remain poor. Seventy-nine percent of unorganised or informal workers belong to India's poor and vulnerable group (NCEUS, 2007).

For the poor, contributing to a pension scheme creates welfare loss as they have very little income in their hands to support even the necessities of life (Holzzmann et al., 2000). The argument in favour relates to the high mortality rate of poor people during old age. Due to this fact, they do not want to defer the consumption of their income by contributing to the pension scheme since they are not sure whether they will be alive in those advancing years of life. This contributes to another reason for low social security in the informal sector and planning for the old-age security in the informal sector.

In addition to this, most poor people in this sector still give more importance to the old system of social security. This relates to having big families or having a male child for their support in the old age (Hoddinott, 1992). They also depend on remittances from their family members who migrate to different places (e.g., Lucas and Stark, 1985; Hoddinott, 1992). Other reasons for the non-participation of informal workers relate to laws which don't make mandatory enrolment of workers to any social security schemes (e.g., EPS/EPF) if the total number of employees is less than 20 in India. Sometimes, the pension fund's return is lower (e.g., EPFO) than the market return. Contributory pension schemes (e.g., NPS-Lite/Swavalmban) are not backed by any government-guaranteed minimum pension amount therefore, workers do not find the schemes advantageous. Some research has also mentioned that the mis-selling of financial products in the microfinance industry in Andhra Pradesh in 2010 may have impacted the participation in contributory pension schemes with similar concerns (Sane and Thomas, 2014).

4.3 Financial Literacy and Retirement Planning

With the development of the economy and financial markets, people have been experiencing more complex financial products than ever before. Therefore, people need to be more aware of the financial markets and the available products. Financial literacy is essential for securing the aptitudes and complexity required to make appropriate financial choices.

Pension markets throughout the World are witnessing a shift from conventional defined benefit (DB) pension plans to private defined contribution (DC) plans due to fiscal pressure, improved life expectancy and other social welfare measures. India, too is not an exception and introduced the National Pension System (NPS) in 2004 for government employees and later for all the citizens and unorganised sector workers (detailed discussion provided in the previous chapter). In old-age security, the decision-making process is more complex due to its long-term nature of investment and uncertainty of the future.

Conventional economic theory suggests that an entirely rational individual will consume less than his/her earnings and save for the future to support his/her consumption after retirement (Lusardi and Mitchell, 2014). Since old-age savings are shifting from employers to employees, they are currently more responsible for their own personal old-age savings after retirement for their longevity risk (Lusardi, 2019).

Several researchers have studied the link between financial literacy and economic behaviours. One of the pioneer research studies to highlight the absence of financial knowledge was Bernheim (1995) on the US households that lacked basic financial knowledge.

Agarwal et al. (2009) show that financial mistakes are most predominant among the young and elderly, groups that also display strikingly low levels of financial knowledge. Financial ignorance has significant bearings on the outcome of wealth and costs. Stango and Zinman (-2007) show that those who are not able to calculate interest rates out of a stream of payments correctly end up borrowing more and accumulating lower amounts of wealth which is a consequence of inadequate financial knowledge. Van Rooij et al. (2007) find that financially sophisticated households are more likely to participate in the stock market.

In the United States, it is found that as many as one-third of the respondents had not thought about retirement at all, which impacted the retirement planning (Lusardi, 1999). The findings for almost a decade later showed no significant improvements, with close to 30% of respondents not having considered saving for retirement (Lusardi and Beeler, 2007; Lusardi and Mitchell, 2007). The major reason individuals refrained from retirement planning is that they were not financially literate.

Lusardi (2008) classified financial literacy as either primary or advanced. The minimum degree of literacy required for all individuals from any type of background to navigate daily life is called basic level literacy. Basic financial literacy involves issues such as numeracy, compound interest, inflation, time, the value of money and the money illusion. Advanced financial literacy involves stock markets, stocks, mutual funds, bonds, other types of securities, and the interest rate effect on securities, security prices and risk-return relationship issues. Both literacy types fit under the term general financial literacy.

The saving and investment decisions of financially literate individuals have positive impacts on their results, not only during their active work life but also after retirement (Lusardi and Mitchell, 2014). It is also found that financial literacy is positively associated with greater retirement planning and greater retirement wealth accumulation. For example, an improvement in an individual's financial literacy contributes to a higher level of probability of stock market participation and retirement planning in the Netherlands (Van Rooij et al., 2012). More than half the wealth inequality in the United States has been explained through a simulated life-cycle model (Lusardi et al., 2013).

An international compression (Table 4.1) between financial literacy and retirement planning across 15 countries was coordinated by a Lusardi and Mitchell under the project called Financial Literacy around the World or (FLat World) to understand the impact of financial literacy on the individual retirement planning in different economies with varied pension system (Lusardi and Mitchell, 2011c).

Table 4.1 shows the level of financial literacy measured by those answering all three questions correctly, varies sharply from one economy to another. It is as low as 3.7% in Russia to 53.2% in Germany. Across countries, the average of financial literacy is around 30%, which is alarming because most countries included in the FLat World project are developed countries, and those economies have well-developed financial markets.

Financially educated individuals are well informed about pension systems and rules and, therefore, make better investment decisions than a less financially informed individuals. Examining the relationship between financial literacy and retirement in Australia, Agnew

Table 4.1 Comparative Statistics from the Flat-World Project across 15 Countries

Authors	Country	Year of Data	Interest Rate		Inflation		Risk Diversification		All 3 Correct (%)	At Least 1 Don't Know (%)	Number of Observations
			Correct (%)	DK (%)	Correct (%)	DK (%)	Correct (%)	DK (%)			
Lusardi and Mitchell (2011c)	USA	2009	64.9	13.5	64.3	14.2	51.8	33.7	30.2	42.4	1,488
Alessie et al. (2011)	Netherlands	2010	84.8	8.9	76.9	13.5	51.9	33.2	44.8	37.6	1,665
Bucher-Koenen and Lusardi (2011)	Germany	2009	82.4	11.0	78.4	17.0	61.8	32.3	53.2	37.0	1,059
Sekita (2011)	Japan	2010	70.5	12.5	58.8	28.6	39.5	56.1	27.0	61.5	5,268
Agnew et al. (2013)	Australia	2012	83.1	6.4	69.3	13.0	54.7	37.6	42.7	41.3	1,024
Crossan et al. (2011)	New Zealand	2009	86.0	4.0	81.0	5.0	27.0	2.0*	24.0*	7.0	850
Brown and Graf (2013)	Switzerland	2011	79.3	2.8*	78.4	4.2*	73.5*	13.0*	50.1*	16.9*	1,500
Fornero and Monticone (2011)	Italy	2007	40.0*	28.2*	59.3*	30.7*	52.2*	33.7*	24.9*	44.9*	3,992

(*Continued*)

Authors	Country	Year of Data	Interest Rate		Inflation		Risk Diversification		All 3 Correct (%)	At Least 1 Don't Know (%)	Number of Observations
			Correct (%)	DK (%)	Correct (%)	DK (%)	Correct (%)	DK (%)			
Almenberg and Säve-Söderbergh (2011)	Sweden	2010	35.2*	15.6*	59.5	16.5	68.4	18.4	21.4*	34.7*	1,302
Arrondel et al. (2013)	France	2011	48.0*	11.5*	61.2	21.3	66.8*	14.6	30.9*	33.4*	3,616
Klapper and Panos (2011)	Russia	2009	36.3*	32.9*	50.8*	26.1*	12.8*	35.4*	3.7*	53.7*	1,366
Beckmann (2013)	Romania	2011	41.3	34.4	31.8*	40.4*	14.7	63.5	3.8*	75.5*	1,030
Moure (2016)	Chile	2009	47.4	32.1	17.7	20.9	40.6	N.A	7.7	53.1	14,463
Boisclair et al. (2017)	Canada	2012	77.9	8.8	66.18	16.13	9.36	31.29	42.5	37.23	6,805
Kalmi and Ruuskanen (2017)	Finland	2014	58.1	6.1	76.5	6.4	65.8	10.25	35.6	14	1,477

Source: Lusardi (2019).
Note: *indicates questions that have slightly different wording than the baseline financial literacy question.

et al. (2013) found that with financial literacy, the probability of pension investment planning increases. Another study also found that employees who were the least financially educated were 34% less likely to participate voluntarily in pension investment planning (Agnew et al., 2007). A positive causal effect of financial literacy or knowledge has been found on retirement planning in the Netherlands too (Alessie et al., 2011). One additional answer to the financial literacy question led to a 10% higher probability of retirement planning in the Netherlands (Mitchell and Lusardi, 2015). It has been found that those who plan can create two to three times more wealth at the time of retirement than those who do not plan for the same (Lusardi and Mitchell, 2011a). Therefore, planning is a significant factor in creating the financial wealth of an individual after retirement.

Almenberg and Säve-Söderbergh (2011) examined the relationship between financial literacy and retirement planning of Swedish adults. They found significant differences in financial literacy between planners and non-planners. Financial literacy levels were found lower among older people, women and those with low education or earnings. Klapper and Panos (2011) investigated the impact of financial literacy on the retirement saving in Russia. They found that higher literacy is positively related to retirement planning and investigating in private pension funds.

The recent OECD findings of the adult literacy among the G20 countries (OECD, 2017) also found similar results of the Flat world project. The OECD study found that the average financial literacy score of the G20 countries is just 12.7 out of a possible 21. France (14.9), Norway (14.6), Canada (14.6) and China (14.1) are the only four G20 countries that achieved a score above 14 whilst four scores below 12 (India, Argentina, Italy and Saudi Arabia).

Exploring the financial literacy researchers also found a definite relationship between socioeconomic and demographic variables and financial literacy. For instance, education plays an important role in financial planning or wealth accumulation. The asset growth of a household with a college education was found much higher than the asset growth of a household with less than high school degree (Poterba et al., 2013). It was found that individuals with low educational levels are less likely to answer the questions correctly (Lusardi and Mitchell, 2011b). Women are found to have lower financial literacy levels, in general, than men and they are less likely to answer the financial literacy questions correctly and have greater difficulty in performing financial calculations (Chen and Volpe, 1998; Lusardi and Mitchell, 2011b). Low-income levels are found to be associated with lower level of financial Literacy (Atkinson and Messy, 2011). Researchers found that financial literacy is low among young and elderly individuals and it poses a hump shape curve during the life time of an individual (Agarwal et al., 2009; Lusardi and Mitchell, 2011c). But then again, Agnew et al. (2013) found that both financial literacy and retirement planning continue to improve with age.

The Standard and Poor's Global Financial Literacy Survey (S&P Global Fin Lit Survey) found that around the World, 33% of adults are having basic financial understanding monetarily, however, there are large variations among nations and groups. Characteristically, 55% of adults in the major advanced economies (Canada, France, Germany, Italy, Japan, the United Kingdom and the United States) are financially literate, whereas BRICS countries (Brazil, Russia, India, China and South Africa) have 28% of adults who are financially literate. The adult literacy in India is only 24% (Klapper et al., 2014).

Very few research has been carried out in developing countries like India. Cole et al. (2011) measured the level and predictors of financial literacy, and its relationship to demand for financial services in India. They found strong relationships between financial literacy and financial behaviour. Their survey data establishes that financial literacy is an important correlate of household financial behaviour and household wellbeing. Agarwal et al. (2010) evaluated the financial literacy of online Indian investors of Hyderabad city. The findings suggest that participants are generally financially literate. Variations in financial literacy levels were observed across demographic and socioeconomic groups.

A recent survey of financial literacy among students, young employees and retired people in India reveals that financial literacy is not extensive. There is a lack of understanding about compound interest, inflation and diversification in investments. It is found that only less than a quarter population has adequate knowledge on financial matters (Agarwalla et al., 2012).

Financial education empowers individuals to take their financial decisions in a better way. Previous research on financial literacy has indicated that levels of financial literacy worldwide are inadmissibly low. Developing nations have significantly less monetarily educated populace when contrasted with developed nations. In India additionally the degree of financial literacy is exceptionally low.

Unorganised sector workers do not want to participate in these schemes for many reasons, including earning below the minimum wage rate. Some researchers have highlighted that the present NPS is doubtful for the low-income workers whose share in the total unorganised workforce maybe around 50% (Ahuja, 2003). Some have argued that the design of the NPS schemes or features of these schemes have failed to attract unorganised sector workers (Rajsekhar et al., 2016). Some researchers argued to introduce a universal pension plan for all the working population in the unorganised sector of India due to the low coverage of present old-age security available in India (Sanyal and Singh, 2013). The fiscal pressure of civil servant pension payments has become a major issue before all the governments and India is not an exception . Therefore, other researchers have suggested a careful and common-sense parametric reforms to improvement on the civil servants' pension (Asher, 2000). Analysing the NPS, Sane and Thomas (2014), has highlighted the lack of investment choices and low transparency in the schemes and argued to improve the investment choice, portability and a rational focus on managing the NPS at low cost. Another study found that future financial concern and financial advice are very important factors that influence the decision-making of individuals (Amlan and Shrutikeerti, 2016).

Assessment of the research referenced above uncovers the obstacles that may arise if we follow a standardised approach for measuring financial literacy worldwide. This is so because of the presence of heterogeneity across nations. The distinction as for various financial set ups, population and occupation structures, literacy levels, age patterns, etc., need to be considered to arrive at accurate results on a country's financial literacy levels. Though the financial education is found to be less effective for low-income people and lower-middle-income economies (Kaiser and Lukas, 2017), other researchers have advocated the promotion of financial and pension literacy in India (Asher, 2007).

Since the informal or unorganised sector workers are not under any old-age pension cover for many reasons, major being earning low level of income to support present consumption and low level of financial literacy due to lower formal education, raises huge concern for the survival and development of this population in old age. Realising the importance of this issue, the present study has tried to find out the participation of the informal sector in the contributory pension schemes under the NPS in India. The book aims to understand how informal workers contribute towards securing future income for their old age concerning different aspects of their financial decision-making behaviour.

5   Primary Survey into Unorganised Sector Pension

A Case of MSMEs in India

5.1 MSME: Definition and Characteristics

Micro, Small and Medium Enterprises (MSMEs) are operating in different areas across the country, particularly in the rural and underdeveloped areas, inter alia, providing enormous job opportunities to the large section of unskilled and semi-skilled workers for the last few decades. MSMEs are contributing immeasurably in the socio-economic development of India by providing equal job opportunities to the semi-skilled or unskilled people with comparatively low capital investments than large industries. MSMEs are working as an ancillary to the large industry by bridging the supply chain gap. Over the years, MSMEs have grown and up-graded themselves with modern technology and infrastructure for the competitive global business environment by producing a diverse range of innovative products and services.

In defining the MSMEs, different economies have used dissimilar parameters. The Government of India has enacted the Micro, Small and Medium Enterprises Development (MSMED) Act, 2006 and defined the MSMEs based on investment separately for manufacturing industries and service industries as follows:

Manufacturing Enterprises (production, processing or preservation of goods):

Micro enterprise: The investment in plant and machinery does not exceed ₹25 lakhs;

Small enterprise: The investment in plant and machinery is more than ₹25 lakhs but does not exceed ₹5 crores;

Medium enterprise: The investment in plant and machinery is more than ₹5 crores but does not exceed ₹10 crores.

DOI: 10.4324/9781003306573-5

In case of the above enterprises, investment in plant and machinery is the original cost excluding land and building and the items specified by the Ministry of Small Scale Industries vide its notification No.S.O.1722 (E) dated 5 October 2006.

Service Enterprises (providing or rendering of services)

Micro enterprise: The investment in equipment does not exceed ₹10 lakhs;
Small enterprise: The investment in equipment is more than ₹10 lakhs but does not exceed ₹2 crores;
Medium enterprise: The investment in equipment is more than ₹2 crores but does not exceed ₹5 crores.

In case of the above enterprises the investment in equipment (original cost excluding land and building and furniture, fittings and other items not directly related to the service rendered or as may be notified under the MSMED Act, 2006; Table 5.1).

To revive the Covid-19 hit economy and extend various support to the MSMEs through various government schemes, the definition of MSMEs was first revised and announced in the Aatma Nirbhar Bharat package on 13th May 2020. Later the same was modified further upwardly and notified with Government of India Gazette Notification S.O. 2119 (E) dated 26 June 2020.

The new definition does not make any difference between the manufacturing and service sectors, instead along with investment a new criterion, Turnover is introduced.

Table 5.1 Classification of MSMEs in India

Type of MSMEs	Old Classification (Act of 2006) (INR-₹)		New Classification (Act of 2020) (All Enterprises) (INR-₹)	
	Manufacturing	Service	Investment	Turnover
Micro enterprise	0–25 lakhs	10 lakhs	Up to 1 Cr. (10 million)	Up to 5 Cr. (50 million)
Small enterprise	25 lakhs to 5 Cr	10 lakhs to 2 Cr	Up to 10 Cr (100 million)	Up to 50 Cr (500 million)
Medium enterprise	5 Cr to 10 Cr	2 Cr to 5 Cr	Up to 50 Cr (500 million)	Up to 250 Cr (2500 million)

Source: https://pib.gov.in/PressReleasePage.aspx?PRID=1628925.

According to the new classification, an enterprise shall be classified as an MSME on the basis of the following criteria of investment and turnover:

Micro enterprise: The investment in plant and machinery or equipment does not exceed ₹1 crore and turnover does not exceed ₹5 crores;

Small enterprise: The investment in plant and machinery or equipment does not exceed ₹10 crore and turnover does not exceed ₹50 crores; and

Medium enterprise: The investment in plant and machinery or equipment does not exceed ₹50 crores and turnover does not exceed ₹250 crores.

5.2 Development of MSMEs in India

With the development and expansion of MSMEs in rural and backward areas, inter alia, providing job opportunities to the section of the society helps in reducing regional imbalances and improving equitable distribution of national income and wealth. India has around 633.88 lakhs (63.39 million) number of unincorporated non-agriculture MSMEs engaged in different economic activities, such as 19.67 million in Manufacturing, 23.04 million in Trade and 20.69 million in Other Services. Importantly, out of total 63.39 million MSMEs, more than half of that (51.25%) is in the rural India. These rural MSMEs along with all other MSMEs play a vital role of proving jobs to the working class (Table 5.2).

Micro enterprises contribute largely to the MSMEs. Out of the total 63.39 million MSMEs, 63.052 million (630.52 lakhs) are micro enterprises that employ less than ten numbers of workers per unit. Again, little more than 51% of micro enterprises are in the rural areas which

Table 5.2 Estimated Number of MSMEs in India (Activity Wise) (in Million)

Category	Rural (in Million)	Urban (in Million)	Total (in Million)	Share (%)
Manufacturing	11.414	8.250	19.665	31
Trade	10.871	12.164	23.035	36
Other Services	10.200	10.485	20.685	33
Electricity	0.003	0.001	0.004	0
All	32.488	30.900	63.388	100

Source: Annual Report 2020–21, MoMSME. https://msme.gov.in/. (1million = 10 lakhs).

Table 5.3 Number of MSMEs in India (in Lakhs)

	Micro	Small	Medium	Total	Share (%)
Rural	324.09	0.78	0.01	324.88	51
Urban	306.43	2.53	0.04	309.00	49
All	630.52	3.31	0.05	633.88	100

Source: Annual Report 2020–21, MoMSME. https://msme.gov.in/. (10 lakhs = 1 million).

are very crucial for augmenting and promoting employment in the rural areas (Table 5.3).

State of Uttar Pradesh (UP) has the highest number of MSMEs in this country with 8.99 million (89.99 lakhs) of units followed by West Bengal (WB) with 8.86 million (88.67 lakhs) units. Top ten states accounted for a share of 74.05% of the total estimated number of MSMEs in India.

5.3 Contribution of MSMEs in India

The MSMEs are the backbone of the Indian economy as it offers job opportunity to the vast pool of traditionally skilled or unskilled workers and provides entrepreneurship opportunity in labour-intensive sector in rural and underdeveloped areas. MSMEs have been contributing significantly in the country's GDP by the way of its expansion in the different sectors of economy and producing varied range of products and services to meet domestic demand and meeting the requirements of the global market. The contribution of MSMEs in the Gross Value Added (GVA) and share in total GDP is increasing steadily (Table 5.4). In recent years, the MSMEs sector has shown a higher growth rate than industrial sector and contributes nearly 50% of the country's exports (Table 5.5).

MSME sector has been creating more than 110.99 million of job in the Indian economy. In total, 36.04 million jobs were created in the Manufacturing sector, 38.79 million in Trade and 36.28 million in Other Services. In the rural area, MSMEs have created 49.78 million jobs in different sectors (Table 5.6).

The total employment generation by the MSME sector is 110.99 million and the micro enterprises itself have 107.62 million (97%) employees in India. Forty-five percent of the total employment created by the MSMEs are in rural areas of India (Table 5.7). Out of 110.99 million employees in MSME sector, 84.47 million (76%) are male employees and remaining 26.49 million (24%) are females.

Table 5.4 Share of Gross Value Added (GVA) of MSME in all India GDP

Year	Share of MSME in GVA (%)	Share of MSME in All India GDP (%)
2014–15	31.80	29.34
2015–16	32.28	29.48
2016–17	32.24	29.25
2017–18	32.79	29.75
2018–19	33.50	30.27

Source: Annual Report 2020–21, MoMSME. https://msme.gov.in/.

Table 5.5 Share of MSMEs Export in Total Export (in Million)

Year	Total Export (US $)	Export by MSMEs (US $)	Share of MSMEs (%)
2012–13	300,400	127,992	42.60
2013–14	314,415	133,313	42.40
2014–15	310,352	138,896	44.75
2015–16	262,291	130,769	49.85
2016–17	275,852	137,068	49.68
2017–18	303,376	147,390	48.58
2018–19	330,000	158,730	48.10

Source: RBI and PIB; https://pib.gov.in/Pressreleaseshare.aspx?PRID=1579757.

Table 5.6 Employment in the MSME Sector (Activity Wise) (in Lakhs)

Category	Rural (in Million)	Urban (in Million)	Total (in Million)	Share (%)
Manufacturing	186.56	173.86	360.41	32
Trade	160.64	226.54	387.18	35
Other Services	150.53	211.69	362.22	33
Electricity	0.06	0.02	0.07	0
All	497.78	612.10	1,109.89	100

Source: Annual Report 2020–21, MoMSME. https://msme.gov.in/. (10 lakhs = 1 million).

Table 5.7 Share of Employment in MSMEs (Rural &
Urban) in India (in Lakhs)

	Micro	Small	Medium	Total	Share (%)
Rural	489.3	7.9	0.6	497.8	45
Urban	568.9	24.1	1.2	612.1	55
All	1,076.2	32.0	1.8	1,109.9	100

Source: Annual Report 2020–21, MoMSME. https://msme.gov.
in/.

5.4 Present Condition of MSMEs in India

The Covid-19 pandemic has hit the MSMEs sector and it has been
one of the most vulnerable sectors because of its nature and its size of
business, high labour-intensive system and lack of financial resources
or avenues. Govt. of India has introduced the "Atmnirbhar Bharat"
package on 13th May 2020 and launched a special scheme, Emergency
Credit Line Guarantee Scheme (ECLGS) in view of Covid-19 crisis to
provide 100% guarantee coverage to banks, NBFCs so that they can
extend the emergency credit facilities to MSMEs to meet their additional term loan or working capital requirements in Covid-19 situation till March 2022. The government has operationalised Rs. 3,00,000
crores (US $ 40.85 billion) collateral-free loan scheme which is likely
to benefit 45 lakh MSMEs. Budget allocation for MSMEs in FY 2022
increased more than doubled to Rs. 15,700 crores (US $ 2.14 billion)
from Rs. 7,572 crores (US $ 1.03 billion) in FY 2021. The MSME min-
istry, in order to strengthen the backbone of the country, targets to
increase its contribution towards GDP by up to 50% by 2025 as India
moves ahead to become a $5 trillion economy (MoMSME, 2020–21).

MSMEs are being encouraged to market and sell their products
through the Government e-Marketplace (GEM) portal which is run
by the government and all the Ministries and public sector undertak-
ings are source their procurement. Ministry of MSME (MoMSME)
has been organising a number of capacity-building skill development
programmes for the existing and potential entrepreneurs to fill the gap
of skilled workforce for the MSME sector (MoMSME, 2020–21).

5.5 Primary Survey into MSME Sector

The informal sector is not under social security cover for many reasons,
with major being earning a low-income level to support present consumption and low level of formal education. This raises huge concerns

for the survival and development of this population in old age. Realising the importance of this issue, this survey (study) aims to find out the awareness level (financial literacy) of the unorganised sector and their participation towards contributory pension Schemes in India under the National Pension System (NPS). We aim to understand how people contribute towards securing future income for their old age with respect to different aspects of their financial decision-making. To date, there are no such studies available in this area to explore the financial behaviour of the informal/unorganised sector in India regarding their old age security or participation in defined contribution pensions. This would be a first of its kind to explore and analyse the financial behaviour of the unorganised sector. Therefore the objective of this section is to understand the financial decision-making behaviour of informal sector workers towards their retirement planning.

5.5.1 *Survey Management and Methodology*

Careful planning is pivotal to the prudent completion of any project which is based on primary survey data. At the early stage of a survey, an extensive literature review helps to conceptualise potential problems and pave the approach of the survey work (Warwick and Lininger, 1975). After the identification of the research/project objective, it is important to formalise a well-constructed questionnaire for a survey. The pilot survey starts just after the first development of the questionnaire, and the initial draft of the questionnaire is usually revised many times based on the inputs and experiences of the pilot survey (Iarossi, 2006).

To contemplate the connection between monetary proficiency (financial behaviour) and retirement planning for their old age security (longevity risk) of the unorganised sector in India, the project has been carried out on the basis of a primary survey on the MoMSME recognised working-class populace in the unorganised sector of West Bengal, India.

We have considered MSME sector for our study for the following reasons;

First, the MSMEs have been contributing significantly in the country's GDP by the way of its expansion in the different sectors of economy and producing varied range of products and services to meet domestic demand and meeting the requirements of the global market. The MSMEs not only encourage the entrepreneurial activities and business innovations but it also create jobs for the unskilled workers in the economy.

Second, in India, we have around 633.88 lakhs (63.38 million) number of MSME; out of which 630.52 lakhs (63.05 million) are micro enterprises which employ less than ten numbers of workers per unit. More than half of the MSMEs are in the rural areas and contribute to the rural economy.

Total employment in the micro enterprises in India is 1,076.20 lakhs (107.6 million) employees. Therefore, the average number of workers employed in these micro enterprises is around 1.71 per unit (MoMSME, 2020–21). These workers are in general without any formal job contract, seasonal in nature and do not cover under any old age social security.

Third, West Bengal is the home of the second largest number of MSME units in India and has the highest share of total MSMEs with 14% share along with Uttar Pradesh (Table 5.8) (MoMSME, 2020–21).

The sampled population comprises about 572,458 workers in the unorganised sector of West Bengal (WB) employed under different clusters among the 278 identified clusters all over WB as reported by the MSME on their official website as of December 2019. MSME has defined a cluster as: "A cluster is a group of enterprises located within an identifiable, manageable and contiguous area where stake-holders producing same/similar products/services to maintain assertive enterprising characters like similar or different methods of production/ quality control/testing/energy consumption/pollution control/technology and

Table 5.8 Comparative MSME Distribution of Top Ten States in India

Sl. No.	States/UT	Number of Units (in Lakhs)	Share (%)
1	Uttar Pradesh	89.99	14
2	West Bengal	88.67	14
3	Tamil Nadu	49.48	8
4	Maharashtra	47.78	8
5	Karnataka	38.34	6
6	Bihar	34.46	6
7	Andhra Pradesh[a]	33.87	5
8	Gujarat	33.16	5
9	Rajasthan	26.87	4
10	Madhya Pradesh	26.74	4
11	Total of above ten states	469.4	74
12	Other States/UTs	164.5	26
13	All	633.9	100

Source: Annual Report 2020–21, MoMSME. https://msme.gov.in/.
[a]Including Telangana.

marketing strategies/setting up of Common Facility Centre is required to supplement the critical activities".[1]

The responses were recorded with the assistance of a questionnaire intended to investigate the financial decision-making behaviour of the unorganised sector towards financial products in India. Our main objective behind designing the sampling method was to include all the geographical locations alongside maximising the representation of different types of sectors. The project was conducted during the latter half of 2019 to mid of 2021.

5.5.2 Sampling Procedure

The power of sampling is the ability to approximate the characteristics of the whole population from a small group within a known margin of error. An opinion poll of approximately 1,000 individuals can be a reasonable measure of public opinion for a population as large as India's/China's, if proper sampling procedures are followed (Iarossi, 2006).

In our survey of unorganised sector workers of MSME sector where the total population is known, and the whole population is spread all over West Bengal, India, we have considered a multistage sampling procedure to collect our primary data. Considering the administrative division of WB, the 23 distinguished districts of WB are divided into five broad districts (as on December 2019). To constitute the sampling frame, these broad divisions were considered to be the first stage strata. Each stratum consists of either four or five districts with unequal population size and unequal total cluster sectors. Table 5.9 represents the five divisions of WB with the districts and the total population and sectors in each division. The clusters present in WB are broadly categorised into 17 sectors, as shown in Table 5.10.

The clusters are not uniformly distributed all over the state, West Bengal, hence based on the working-class population in the particular sector in each district, the method of proportional allocation was adapted to collect the responses. Table 5.11 provides us with the respective working population of MSME workers in each district with a total number of different MSME clusters available in those districts.

5.5.3 Calculation of Sample Size

In this survey, the total population (that is N is known) is known; therefore, we have used the Cochran's sample size formula (Cochran, 1977) for known population size,

Table 5.9 MSME Population Based on Administrative Division of West Bengal

Sl.No.	Administrative Division	Districts	MSME Population	MSME Sectors
1	JALPAIGURI	Alipurduar Coochbehar Darjeeling Jalpaiguri Kalimpong	26,775	35
2	BARDDHAMAN	Purba Barddhaman Paschim Barddhaman Birbhum Hoogly	56,188	35
3	PRESIDENCY	Kolkata North 24 Parganas South 24 Parganas Howrah Nadia	356,067	78
4	MALDAH	Uttar Dinajpur Dakshin Dinajpur Murshidabad Maldah	38,480	58
5	MEDINIPUR	Purba Medinipur Paschim Medinipur Jhargram Bankura Purulia	94,948	72

Source: https://wb.gov.in.

$$n_0 = \frac{Z^2 pq}{e^2} \tag{5.1}$$

where e = margin of error/desired level of precision

p = The estimated proportion of the population which has the attribute in question.

$$q = 1 - p$$

z value found in *Z*-table with respect to the confidence interval.

n_0 = The determining sample size

Table 5.10 Different Clusters of MSME Sectors in WB

Sl. No.	Cluster Sector
1	Food product and processing
2	Leather and allied products
3	Clay and ceramic
4	Metal fabrication and furniture
5	Textile and readymade garments
6	Jute and other fibre-based products
7	Chemical product other than plastic
8	Wooden furniture and allied products
9	Plastic products
10	Transport equipment and parts
11	Jewellery
12	Basic metal and alloy industry
13	Assembling and servicing
14	Printing
15	Optical lenses grinding
16	Electricals
17	Machinery and equipment other than transport

Source: https://wbmsme.gov.in/msmecluster.

Table 5.11 District wise MSME Worker Population and Number of MSME Cluster Sectors. In West Bengal, India

Sl. No	Division	Districts	Population	Sectors
1	JALPAIGURI	Alipurduar	3,471	3
		Coochbehar	1,363	8
		Darjeeling	10,759	15
		Jalpaiguri	10,87	3
		Kalimpong	10,095	6
2	BARDDHAMAN	Purba Barddhaman	20,040	4
		Paschim Barddhaman	11,158	4
		Birbhum	3,940	13
		Hoogly	21,050	14
3	PRESIDENCY	Kolkata	79,060	6
		North 24 Parganas	15,426	22
		South 24 Parganas	116,656	10
		Howrah	126,790	25
		Nadia	18,135	15
4	MALDAH	Uttar Dinajpur	10,542	17
		Dakshin Dinajpur	1,010	2
		Murshidabad	15,654	21
		Maldah	11,274	18
5	MEDINIPUR	Purba Medinipur	76,497	22
		Paschim Medinipur	2,758	17
		Jhargram	373	3
		Bankura	9,256	16
		Purulia	60,264	14

Source: https://wbmsme.gov.in/msmecluster.

If n_0 / N is negligible where N = population size, then we go for n_0. Otherwise we use the Cochran's correction formula for known sample size.

correction formula:

$$n = \frac{n_0}{1 + \frac{(n_0 - 1)}{N}} \qquad (5.2)$$

For our data:

Population size = 572,458, confidence intervals 95% and margin of error =3%, therefore Z value is 1.96. Therefore sample size is 1,067. We did not use the correction formula because the ratio n_0 / N was negligible, and also, the sample size of 1,067 is less than 5% of the total population.

Considering a confidence interval of 95% and margin of error to be 3% for a population of size 572,458, the sample size is 1,067 by using Cochran's sample size determination formula. Since the population size for each stratum is known, using proportional allocation, we have found out the sample size for each stratum (Table 5.12). We have, involuntarily, not used optimal allocation because the average cost per sample for each stratum was unknown. Neyman's allocation, which considers the size of strata and variability, was avoided because the variation in the stratum sample sizes was too heterogeneous. Therefore, we have used proportional allocation because the population size of each stratum is unequal. The proportional allocation formula is as follows:

$$n_h = \frac{n}{N} N_h, \quad \text{where } N = \text{Population size} \qquad (h = 1, 2, 3, 4, 5)$$
$$n = \text{Sample size}$$
$$N_h = \text{Stratum population size}$$
$$n_h = \text{Stratum sample size}$$

Now each of the districts in the respective divisions is ranked from 1 to 4 or 5, concerning the number of districts present in the division. The rank of the districts (Table 5.13) is calculated on weightage based on the number of cluster sectors present in that particular district to the total number of cluster sectors present in that division. The first ranked district was the chosen district to collect our sample. This method has been used to collect data from the district with the highest number of clusters for better representation of the whole MSME sectors.

The following weightage formula has been used to rank the districts based on clusters:

$$W_t = \frac{\text{Number of sectors in the } t\text{th district}}{\text{Total number of sectors in the division}}, \quad t = 1, 2, ..., 5$$

Table 5.12 Proportional Allocation of Sample in Each
Division

Division	Population (N_h)	Sample (n_h)
Jalpaiguri	26,775	50
Barddhaman	56,188	105
Presidency	356,067	663 (actually 663.6~664)
Maldah	38,480	72
Medinipur	94,948	177
Total	572,458	1,067[2]

Source: Calculated by the author.

Table 5.13 The Rank of the Districts Based on Weightage

Division	Total Clusters	Districts	No. of Clusters	Weights	Rank
Jalpaiguri	35	Alipurduar	3	0.085	4
		Coochbehar	8	0.229	2
		Darjeeling	15	0.429	1
		Jalpaiguri	3	0.085	4
		Kalimpong	6	0.171	3
Barddhaman	35	Purba Barddhaman	4	0.114	3
		Paschim Barddhaman	4	0.114	3
		Birbhum	13	0.371	2
		Hoogly	14	0.4	1
Presidency	78	Kolkata	6	0.077	5
		North 24 Parganas	22	0.192	2
		South 24 Parganas	10	0.282	4
		Howrah	25	0.128	1
		Nadia	15	0.321	3
Maldah	58	Uttar Dinajpur	17	0.293	3
		Dakshin Dinajpur	2	0.034	4
		Murshidabad	21	0.362	1
		Maldah	18	0.310	2
Medinipur	72	Purba Medinipur	22	0.306	1
		Paschim Medinipur	17	0.236	2
		Jhargram	3	0.042	5
		Bankura	16	0.222	3
		Purulia	14	0.194	4

Source: Calculated by the author.

The selected districts are Darjeeling from Jalpaiguri division, Hoogly from Barddhaman division, Howrah from Presidency division, Murshidabad from Maldah division and Purba Medinipur from Medinipur division.

The selected districts in each division have different sectors (varies from district to district). To find out how many respondents we should collect (i.e. sample to be collected) from each sector, we perform proportional allocation based on the population size of the individual sectors. If a cluster sector is present more than once, we took the area with maximum employees. If more than one area is present with the same number of employees, we consider an area after performing simple random sampling without replacement to minimise the error in randomness. The selected clusters in each district with the required sample representation or size have been calculated (Table 5.14) for the collection of our survey data, which we conducted in the early phase of 2020 (January to March) and then from December 2020 to March 2021. We couldn't conduct our survey work throughout 2020 due to the Covid-19 pandemic.

5.5.4 Collection of Responses

To conduct the survey, we have conducted a pilot survey in the Bardhaman District of West Bengal with a preliminary questionnaire based on the inputs from the existing literature in the pension research. After conducting the pilot survey and based on the feedback received during the survey, we have modified our questionnaire and redrafted for our final use (INFE, 2011). The final questionnaire comprises a total of 42 questions (developed in three languages viz; Bengali, Hindi and English) ranging from demographic features of the respondent to questions designed to understand the financial knowledge and financial behaviour of the participants of the unorganised sector workers in India. Bengali is the local language, and most of the workers speak Bengali as their primary language. Hindi is the most common language for communication in India, and also it has been used as an official language recently along with English. We collected a dataset throughout the West Bengal, based on the selected districts and clusters (Table 5.14), through face-to-face interviews of 730 respondents and refined the data set based on the available answered questions. We could not achieve our desired target of 1,067 respondents due to lockdown throughout the country due to the sudden outbreak of Covid-19 pandemic in India and rest of the world as well. After the reopening of the first lockdown, we once again started our field work and could

Table 5.14 Sample Size of Respective Clusters in Each Selected Districts in West Bengal

District	Sector	Total Units	Employees (Population)	Total Employees (Population)	Sample
Darjeeling	FPP	5	2,000	7,594	13
	LAP	1	180		1
	CC	1	250		2
	MFF	1	300		2
	TRG	3	504		3
	JF	1	160		1
	CP	2	4,000		26
	WP	1	200		1
					*** Total is 49, so we have to adjust one.
Hoogly	LAP	1	330	18,310	2
	CC	1	360		2
	TRG	4	1,200		7
	PP	3	1,000		6
	JEW	1	1,100		6
	BM	1	150		0.8~1
	Pr	1	12,000		69
	OG	1	170		0.9~1
	E	1	2,000		11
Howrah	FPP	1	236	96,526	2
	CC	1	300		2
	MFF	1	165		1
	TRG	4	22,500		156
	JF	4	1,500		10
	CP	1	3,025		21
	WP	1	150		1
	JEW	2	24,000		165
	BM	5	40,000		275
	AS	2	150		1
	OG	2	2,000		14
	ME	1	2,500		17
					** Total is 665 we have to subtract 2.

(Continued)

Murshidabad	FPP	1	140	10,647	1
	CC	4	1,800		12
	MFF	2	2,035		14
	TRG	1	500		3
	JF	2	3,000		20
	WP	3	1,200		8
	PP	3	500		3
	TP	1	420		3
	JEW	2	852		6
	BM	2	200		1
					*** Total coming is 71 so we have to add 1
Purba Medinipur	FPP	2	50,000	70,180	126
	CC	4	2,000		5
	MFF	9	600		2
	TRG	1	1,030		3
	JF	2	15,000		38
	CP	2	800		2
	TP	1	250		1
	BM	1	500		1
					***The total is 177, so we have to discard 1.

collect the required number of respondents just before the second lockdown announced due to the second wave of coronavirus in India.

Notes

1 https://wbmsme.gov.in/cluster-dev-prog.
2 If $p = 0.5$. Now let's say we want 95% confidence, and at least 5% – plus or minus – precision. A 95 % confidence level gives us Z values of 1.96, per the normal tables, so we get $((1.96)2 (0.5) (0.5)) / (0.05)2 = 385$.

Therefore, a random sample of 385 households in our target population should be enough to give us the confidence levels we need (Israel, 1992).

6 Understanding Financial Behaviour of MSME Workers

6.1 Overview of Sample Characteristics

The questionnaire (Annexure: 1) comprises a total of 42 questions (developed in three languages viz; Bengali, Hindi and English) ranging from demographic features of the respondent to questions designed to understand the financial knowledge and financial behaviour of the participants of the unorganised sector workers in India. Bengali is the local language, and most of the workers speak Bengali as their primary language. Hindi is the most common language for communication in India, and also it has been used as an official language recently along with English. We collected a data set throughout the West Bengal, based on the selected districts and clusters through face-to-face interviews of 730 respondents and refined the data set based on the available answered questions. Survey respondents were requested to state their monthly income and monthly household expenses along with education, gender, age and financial questions. But some respondents (10.54%) did not answer all the questions or were reluctant to share all the personal and financial information while interviewing, and therefore few entries were missing. Therefore, we did not consider those responses with incomplete information or data set about the workers. Out of the 730, we find 653 responses[1] (89.45%) were correct and used in our study.

Our sample respondents consist of 87.4% male and 12.5% female unorganised sector workers spread across different income and age groups. Our sample consists of 80% married people, with 19% unmarried and merely 1% are either widow-divorced or separated. The sample respondents of different age groups and income groups are well distributed (normally), which is evident from their distributions charts (Figures 6.1 and 6.2).

The average age of the collected sample of unorganised sector workers at different MSME clusters of West Bengal is at around 46 years

DOI: 10.4324/9781003306573-6

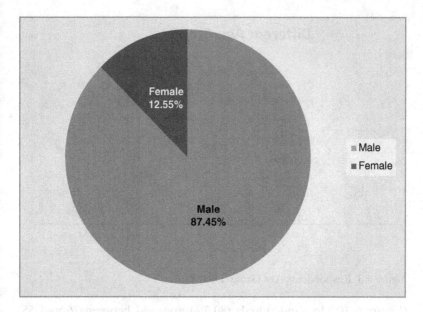

Figure 6.1 Gender Distribution of Sample.

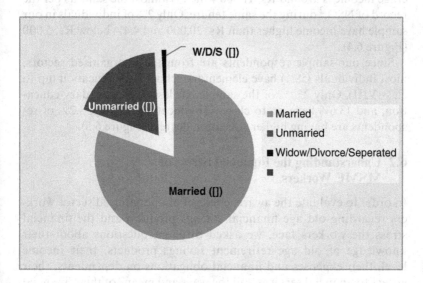

Figure 6.2 Marital Status of Respondents.

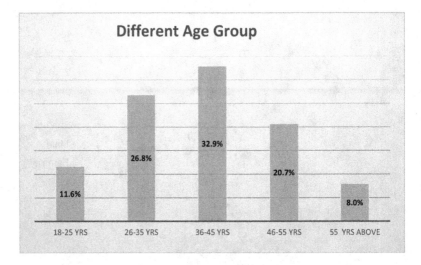

Figure 6.3 Respondents Age Group Distribution.

(Figure 6.3). Most individuals (80.3%) are aged between 26 and 55 years in our sample. More than half of the sample respondents (51.8%) have an income of Rs. 10,000–15,000 per month, and our sample's average income is around Rs. 11,500 which is almost the same as per the record of NSO,[2] during the same tenure. Only 2% of individuals in our sample have income higher than Rs. 20,000 and 4.4% below Rs. 5,000 (Figure 6.4).

Since our sample respondents are from the unorganised sectors, most individuals (58%) have elementary school level education (up to class VIII). Only 25.1% of the sample has less than secondary education, and 13.6% have up to class XII education. Merely, 3.2% of respondents are having higher education degrees (Figure 6.5).

6.2 Understanding the Financial Stress of MSME Workers

In order to evaluate the awareness level of unorganised sector workers regarding old age financial savings products and the financial stress the workers face, we asked different questions about their knowledge of old age retirement savings products, their income level, their expenses and financial obligations on dependents, their access to financial services and the ways and means of their financial habits.

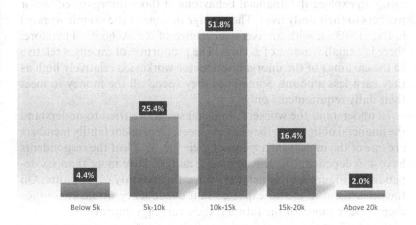

Figure 6.4 Respondent's Income Group Distribution.

Level of Education

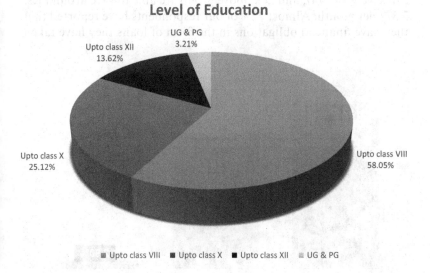

Figure 6.5 Respondent's Educational Level.

Since our sample respondents are widely spread among different income groups and age groups with varied educational levels, it's interesting to explore the financial behaviour of those unorganised sector workers in their daily lives. The average income of the sample workers is Rs. 11,803.21, with an average expense of Rs. 9,666.92. Therefore, there is a small window of savings. The proportion of expenses relative to the earnings of the unorganised sector workers is relatively high as they earn less amount. Sometimes they spend all the money to meet their daily requirements only.

To understand the workers' financial stress, we tried to understand the financial obligations they have to meet. Dependent family members are one of the important aspects of their life. 43.3% of the respondents have 4–6 dependent family members, and 3% have more than six dependents (Figure 6.6), which may surge the monthly expenditure. On the other hand, it is also expected that dependency would encourage them to save more for the future if their earnings improve.

If we look at the average savings of all the different income groups of the sample respondents, we can see the upward trend of higher savings with higher income (Figure 6.7). On average, the income group of 5–10k can save Rs. 1,019, 10–15k can save Rs. 1,652, 15–20K can save Rs. 2,447, and 20k above group are able to save around Rs. 3,377 per month. Almost 22% of our respondents have reported that they have financial obligations in the form of loans they have taken

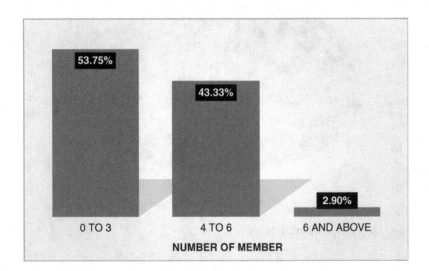

Figure 6.6 Number of Dependents (in %) of Respondents.

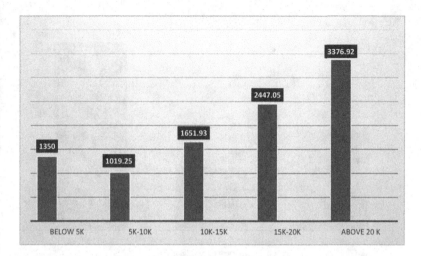

Figure 6.7 Average Savings of Different Income Groups of Respondents.

from different sources. Therefore, the degree of savings decreases with less income which doesn't provide any opportunity to save for obvious reasons of maintaining a basic minimum livelihood. This highlights the financial stress faced by the unorganised sector workers in India.

We have also noticed that the workers are encouraged to save more if they have more dependents in their families. The percentage of savers improves from 12.37% of unorganised sector workers when they have dependents of 4–6 members to almost 37% when their dependent family members increase to 6 and above (Figure 6.8). This is a kind of forced savings that workers are required to maintain to meet the different necessities such as food, health, education, etc.

The finding of forced savings of the workers led us to inquire more into the financial behaviour of the unorganised sector workers to explore why they save and, importantly, how they are saving. Almost 45% of our sample respondents save for their child education, and a similar proportion of respondents save for household requirements (Figure 6.9). This is in line with the savings pattern when they have more dependents. But 21% of respondents also save for heath requirements which is probably the impact of increasing out-of-pocket-expenses (OOPE) in health care in our country. The economic survey (2021) has cited that the high level of OOPE may lead to poverty of the vulnerable section.[3] The workers also save for their future child

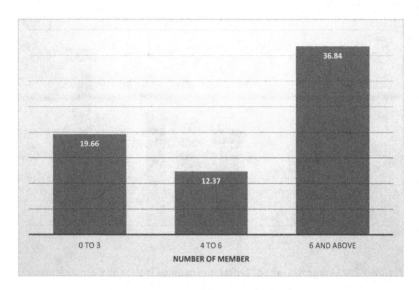

Figure 6.8 Savers Having Dependents.

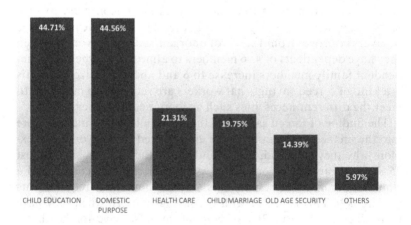

Figure 6.9 Reasons for Savings.

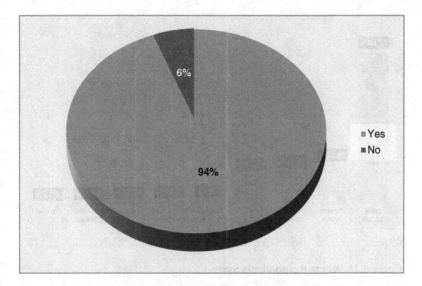

Figure 6.10 Bank Account of the Respondents (in %).

marriage (19.7%). Interestingly, our sample of unorganised sector workers found that 14.3% of workers are recognising the importance of longevity risk and are saving for their old age security.

Therefore, we tried to explore more to know about their modes of saving. This is crucial for our study to know whether they have access to or knowledge about any financial product or not and, specifically, about pension products.

In our sample respondents, most workers (94%) have a bank account or access to financial services (Figure 6.10). This finding reproduces the evidence of an effective policy by the Government of India, namely the Pradhan Mantri Jan Dhan Yojana (PMJDY) in 2015, which tried to ensure that bank accounts for the poor marginalised sections in India. Around 78% of sample respondents save through Bank Account, and almost 21% of workers keep cash as their savings. While 16.3% of workers save through Post Offices, 15.4% of workers invest in life insurance policies for savings (Figure 6.11). Only 0.76% of the respondents are investing in Public Provident Fund and 0.61% in other welfare schemes directly.

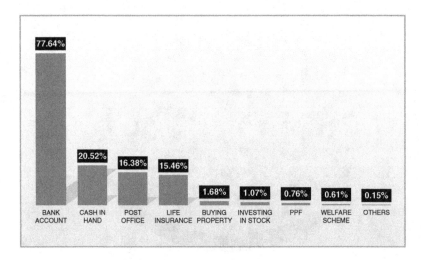

Figure 6.11 Where Respondents Save.

6.3 Awareness Level of the MSME Workers

To know the awareness level of unorganised sector workers regarding the available financial products of old age security or
pension schemes in India, we asked survey participants (MSME
workers) whether they heard about the Atal Pension Yojana
(APY)/Swavalamban or Pradhan Mantri Shram Yogi Maan-Dhan
scheme (PMSYM). Fifty-six percent of the respondents replied
positively about the knowledge of existing contributory pension
schemes in India. This is very encouraging to know that people are
becoming aware of the different financial products available for old
age security (Figure 6.12).

But only 17.21% of the survey participants who knows about the different financial products available for old age security in India invest
in those pension schemes (APY/PMSYM). This is not as encouraging
as the knowledge about pension financial products is witnessed. The
survey also revealed that most of the workers (51%) treat bank deposits
(savings) as their retirement savings. In total, 6.5% of workers keep
hard cash as their old age security, 4.2% of workers invest in life insurance policies as old-age savings and merely, 2.2% invest in gold to
protect themselves from old age requirements. The low investments
in the pension schemes encourage us to study the financial literacy of
unorganised sector workers in India.

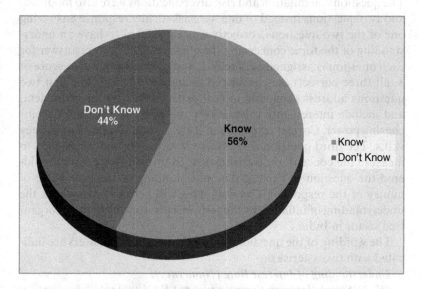

Figure 6.12 Awareness of Pension Schemes by the Unorganised Sector Workers.

6.4 Understanding the Financial Literacy of MSME Workers

Research has revealed that the probability of planning for retirement is extremely correlated with financial literacy (Agnew et al., 2013; Alessie et al., 2011; Almenberg and Säve-Söderbergh, 2011; Bernheim, 1995; Klapper and Panos, 2011; Lusardi and Mitchell, 2007, 2011a).

The evaluation of financial literacy is estimated with three financial literacy questions that address basic economics and finance concepts and is used to append their understanding of interest calculations, the relationship between risk and return, inflation and prices, inflation and return, and the role of diversification in risk reduction. These three financial literacy questions, called the Big Three, were proposed by Lusardi and Mitchell (2011a) and have been every now and again utilised in research especially focused on financial literacy and retirement planning in several countries, including Germany, Italy, Japan, Netherlands, New Zealand Russia, Sweden, and the United States.

The three big questions have been modified from the viewpoint of the Indian context and our target population. To understand the responded numerical knowledge, we started with a fundamental question on simple interest followed by a question on compound interest.

The questions on inflation and risk diversifications were also modified, and two questions instead of one were asked; any response answering one of the two questions correctly was considered to have an understanding of the topic concerning the question. The correct answer for each question is assigned a score of 1, and respondents with a score of 3 (all three correct) are considered financially literate. The first two questions address economic topics related to saving for retirement, and include interest rate calculations and effect of inflation on purchasing power. Correct responses to these questions require numeracy skills. The third question is related to investments and is designed to measure the concept of diversification. In this study, we have considered the question to explore the understanding of the time value of money of the respondents as well. This will help us cross-check the understanding of inflation by the respondents working in the unorganised sector in India.

The wording of the questions is as follows (correct answers are indicated with two asterisks):

Understanding of Interest Rate (Numeracy):

Q1.A) Simple Interest: Suppose you put Rs. 1,000 into a savings account with a guaranteed interest rate of 4% per year. How much would be in the account at the end of the first year, once the interest payment is made?

[Open response: correct answer Rs. 1,040]

Q1.B) Compound Interest: Suppose you have Rs. 200 in a savings account, and the interest is 10% per year. How much will you have in the account after two years? (Amount in Rs)

Exactly 220
Exactly 240
Less than 240
More than 240**
Do not know

Understanding of Inflation.

Q2.A) High Inflation means the cost of living is increasing rapidly?
True**
False

Q2.B) Suppose that in the year 2020, your income has doubled and prices of all goods have doubled too. In 2020, how much will you be able to buy with your income?

More than today
Exactly the same**
Less than today
Do not know

Refuse to answer

Understanding of Risk Diversification.

Q3.A) An investment with a high return is likely to be high risk

True**

False

Do not know

Q3.B) It is less likely that you will lose all of your money if you save it in more than one place

Yes**

No

Understanding of Time Value of Money

Q4.A) Assume a friend inherits Rs. 10,000 today and his sibling inherits Rs. 10,000, three years from now. Who is richer because of the inheritance?

My friend**

His sibling

They are equally rich

Do not know

Refuse to answer

A summary of respondents' answers is provided in Table 6.1. Two asterisk signs denote the correct answer for each question. When we tried to evaluate the numerical knowledge of the respondent with simple interest and compound interest questions, our findings are in quite a contrast with each other. Only 30.62% of respondents could answer the simple interest question (question no. 1.A). The proportion of correct answers decreases considerably, to 9.49%, when we consider the compound interest calculation (question no. 1.B). This was the most challenging question for the unorganised sector workers. They are not good at numeracy, and importantly they lack the knowledge of compounding.

In the case of inflation, 58.6% of respondents could answer the question. When we asked generalised questions on inflation (question no. 2.A), we received surprisingly higher correct answers (86%). The pattern of responses changed affectedly when the question was reconstructed to a little more complex with more words (question no. 2.B). To corroborate the understanding of inflation, we have also asked a question (question no. 4.A) on the time value of money. The results are close to that of the inflation. We could find that 54% of workers understand the concept of the time value of money.

Surprisingly, 78% of the respondents answer correctly to the risk diversification question (question no. 3.A), but the same increases to 90% when we have asked a well-defined simpler form of diversification

Table 6.1 Summary Statistics on Three Financial Literacy
Questions (%)

Sl. No.	Questions	Response in Percentage (%)
1.	Interest question	
	Correct answer**	30.62
	Incorrect answer	69.37
2.	Inflation question	
	More than today	15.92
	Exactly the same**	58.65
	Less than today	15.00
	Do not know	8.11
	Refuse to answer	2.29
3.	Risk diversification question	
	True**	78.25
	False	8.73
	Do not know	13.02
4.	Cross question	
	(Time value of money)	
	My friend**	54.05
	His sibling	14.85
	They are equally rich	23.12
	Do not know	7.04
	Refuse to answer	0.91

Note: Table calculated from the responses of q. no. 1.A for interest, q. no.
2.B for inflation q. no. 3.A for risk diversification and q. no. 4 for time value
of money.
**: Correct answer.

question (question no. 3.B). Overall the financial literacy of Indian
workers from the unorganised sector is not encouraging compared
to that of the developed countries such as the Netherland, Australia,
Russia and Germany (Lusardi and Mitchell, 2014). Since the overall
financial literacy is low, it is essential to analyse more into the fact that
who is more financially literate and who is least among our sample
respondents.

6.5 Who Is Financially Illiterate? Who Is the Least Financially Literate?

Table 6.2 summarises the responses to the financial literacy questions
by sociodemographic characteristics such as age, gender, education
and employment status of the unorganised sector workers in India.
The table reports responses to individual question responses. If we
look at the relationship between education and financial literacy, we

Table 6.2 Distribution of Responses to Financial Literacy Questions by Age, Gender, Education and Employment Status (in %)

	Interest		Inflation		Risk Diversification		Overall 3 Measures		n
	Correct	Incorrect	Correct	Incorrect	Correct	Incorrect	All Correct	At Least 1 Correct	
1 Education									
Up to class VII	18.20	81.79	55.673	44.3271	78.36	21.63	9.76	92.08	379
Up to class X	40.24	59.75	58.537	41.4634	76.82	23.17	18.29	95.12	164
Up to class XII	60.67	39.32	71.91	28.089	79.77	20.22	33.70	96.62	89
UG and above	52.38	47.61	60	40	80.95	19.04	38.09	85.71	21
2 Gender									
Male	32.22	67.77	61.64	38.35	78.80	21.19	16.63	94.39	571
Female	19.51	80.48	37.80	62.19	74.39	25.60	12.19	85.36	82
3 Age									
18–25 years	40.78	59.21	48.68	51.315	75	25	22.36	88.15	76
26–35 years	36	64	62.85	37.14	76	24	18.85	93.14	175
36–45 years	27.44	72.55	58.60	41.39	80.93	19.06	13.48	94.41	215
46–55 years	27.40	72.59	56.29	43.70	81.48	18.51	15.55	95.55	135
55 years above	19	80.76	65.38	34.61	71.15	28.84	9.61	90.38	52
4 Employment status									
Permanent	33.67	66.32	60.20	39.79	77.55	22.44	19.38	93.87	98
Temporary (contractual)	29.88	70.11	59.76	40.23	78.11	21.88	14.11	93.88	425
Self employed	29.16	70.83	39.58	60.41	72.91	27.08	16.66	85.41	48
Daily paid	31.70	68.29	62.19	37.80	82.92	17.07	21.95	93.90	82
Total sample-653									

Note: Complete table with the response of time value of money is provided in the annexure: 2.

find that education is positively correlated with financial literacy. With higher education, people tend to have more financial knowledge, which is consistent with other studies (Alessie et al., 2011). We have different groups of respondents based on different education categories. The first category is elementary school education up to class VII standard. The second category is up to class X level of education. The next category includes individuals with a high school education (up to class XII). The last category includes all the individuals who have higher education (Figure 6.13).

In terms of gender, we found large differences in financial knowledge among male and female respondents. This is in line with the findings of other countries too (Agnew et al., 2013; Alessie et al., 2011; Almenberg and Säve-Söderbergh, 2011; Lusardi and Mitchell, 2008). Men are better in interest calculation and comprehension of inflation. The gap between males and females is wider (23%) in the case of inflation questions, where 61% of male respondents could answer correctly with 38% correct female responses. The gap between males and females in interest calculation is a little smaller (12%) than the inflation question. Remarkably, risk diversification understanding measured well ahead than other countries; in males and females with 91% and 81%, respectively in our sample respondents. Overall, only 19% of males could answer all the financial literacy questions correctly, whereas it is only 12% in the case of women (Figure 6.14). This is probably higher male

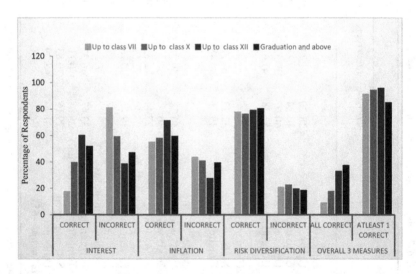

Figure 6.13 Education and Financial Literacy of Respondents (in %).

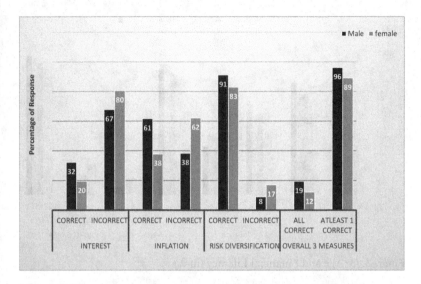

Figure 6.14 Gender and Financial Literacy of Respondents (in %).

literacy in India and less involvement of women in financial decision-making. This result is visible in most countries, including developed countries (Almenberg and Säve-Söderbergh, 2011). One explanation of this phenomenon throughout the world is probably the by and large financial dependence of women on men (Figure 6.14).

It is observed that the relationship between financial literacy and age in India is negatively correlated, which is in line with the findings of Klapper and Panos (2011). We found that the young respondents answer more correctly than older people in every stage of age differences. This is exactly the opposite of the findings of other studies (such as Agnew et al., 2013; Lusardi and Mitchell, 2011c) where younger individuals have a tendency to respond less accurately than their older counterparts. We have used different working-age categories to understand more about their financial behaviour. The unorganised sector workers are categorised under five different groups as 18–25 years, 26–35 years, 36–45 years, 46–55 years and 55 years and above. In the case of interest calculation question, the young respondents (18–25 years) have answered more accurately (41%) than their older age groups. The correct answer percentage reduces with the higher age groups, and the least accuracy (only 19%) was witnessed in the case of 55 years and above age group. This pattern is

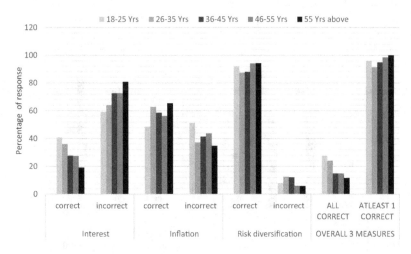

Figure 6.15 Age and Financial Literacy (in %).

manifested when we look at the overall financial literacy of the different age groups.

Last column of Figure 6.15 shows the response of all the respective age group respondents who answered all three questions correctly. Twenty-two percent of the respondents in the age group of 18–25 years answer correctly all the financial literacy questions, where the age group of 55 years and above answered least correctly with 9.6%. We could not find a hump-shaped financial literacy with age as in other studies (Agarwal, 2009; Almenberg and Säve-Söderbergh, 2011), but a downward sloping curve with age has emerged with the overall financial literacy performance of the respondents in India. In the case of comprehending inflation, we found an opposite relation where understanding of inflation increases with age. The plausible explanation of this kind of findings is, one, the literacy rate in India started improving within the last 20–25 years only when the Government of India initiated the Sarva Shiksha Abhiyan (SSA) (Education for All Movement) programme aimed at the universalisation of primary education free and compulsory to children between the ages of 6 and 14. Therefore, the young population have a higher level of education and numerical ability with better financial knowledge (Figure 6.16).

Finally, financial literacy doesn't vary much with the respondents' employment status except for the self-employed workers. Self-employed workers consistently answer all three individual questions

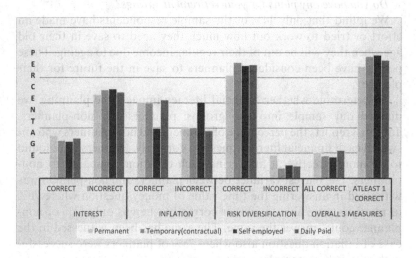

Figure 6.16 Nature of Employment and Financial Literacy of Respondents (in %).

least correctly compared to other groups of respondents. Overall, for all three financial literacy questions, daily paid workers answers were more successful (22%) than permanent workers (19%), self-employed (17%) and temporary workers (14%).

6.6 Retirement Planning and Financial Literacy in India

Since this project's primary objective is to understand the financial decision-making behaviour of unorganised sector workers towards their retirement planning, in this section, we try to explore whether financial literacy relates to retirement planning in India. The existing literature finds that financial literacy does transmit to retirement planning (e.g., Agnew et al., 2013; Almenberg and Säve-Söderbergh, 2011; Behrman et al., 2012 Klapper and Panos, 2011; Lusardi, 2009; Lusardi and Mitchell, 2011a).

In order to assess the impact of financial literacy on retirement planning, we asked respondents from the unorganised sector in India about their retirement planning. The question was little modified from the retirement planning question used in Lusardi and Mitchell's papers (2011a, 2011b). We tried to get a simple "yes" or "no" answer for their planning. We asked them the following question:

Do you have any plans for your retirement savings?

We found that only 14% of the sample respondents have made an effort or tried to work out how much they need to save in their old age when they will be out of their regular income due to ageing. These people have been considered planners to save in the future for their old age.

To determine whether financial literacy impacts the planning, we divided our sample into two groups: planners and non-planners. Table 6.3 reports the percentage of planners and non-planners who answered each financial literacy question correctly. Planners were found to be more effective at answering each question compared to non-planners. The biggest variance between planners and non-planner was witnessed in answering the time value of money question where 70% of planners were able to answer correctly whereas only 51% of non-planner could answer the same. The same has been witnessed in the case of inflation question also where 75% of planners were successful with only 56% of non-planners.

Planners were also better at numeracy (interest calculation question), with little more than 38% of planners could calculate interest (Figure 6.17). Overall, 23% of the planners could answer all the questions correctly (financially literate). The concept of inflation, along with numeracy, is important for future financial planning. In both cases, planners are more successful than non-planners. If we consider

Table 6.3 Financial Literacy of Planner and Non-Planner

Sl. no.	Questions	Planner (%)	Non-Planner
1	Interest Question		
	Correct	38.46	29.35
	Incorrect	61.53	70.64
2	Inflation Question		
	Correct	74.72	56.05
	Incorrect	25.27	43.95
3	Risk Diversification Question		
	Correct	73.62	79.00
	Incorrect	26.38	21
4	Time Value of Money		
	Correct	70.32	51.42
	Incorrect	29.67	48.57
5	Summary		
	Correct: interest and inflation	29.67	17.25
	Correct all three	23.07	14.94
	Correct at least 1	95.6	92.88

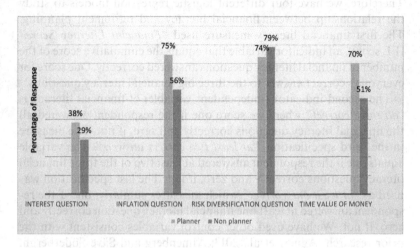

Figure 6.17 Financial Literacy of Planners and Non-Planners (in %).

the interest and inflation questions together, almost 30% of planners were correct, whereas it is only 17% for non-planners.

6.7 Relationship between Pension Planning and Financial Literacy

In this section, we tried to explore the relationship between pension planning of unorganised sector workers and Financial Literacy in India. We have used the retirement planning question indicator as to the dependent variable in our model specification. We asked a simple question that,

Have you ever tried to know how much you need to save for retirement?

Dependent variable *"willing to save"* equals one (1) if respondents answered our retirement planning question favourably and zero otherwise. Since our dependent variable is the binary form (0/1), we have used a binary logistic regression framework to analyse the relationship. We did not use the linear probability model (LPM), which may predict probability in negative or greater than one for some value of the regressors (nonsensical). Therefore, the linearity of the relationship is questionable and improbable to support real-life behaviour.[4] The logit model is a non-linear specification that ensures that the predicted probability lies between 0 and 1.

Four (4) different financial literacy measures were used in our study to measure the impact of financial literacy on retirement planning.

Therefore, we have four different logistic regression models to study the relationship between financial literacy and retirement planning. The first financial literacy measure used *"Financial Literacy Score"* (FL score), an indicator variable that equals the cumulative score of the number of financial literacy questions answered correctly. One score for everyone's correct answer to the three big financial literacy questions.

The second indicator (independent variable) of financial literacy is *"all three correct"* where we score one if the respondent answered all the financial literacy questions correctly and zero, if not. The measure in the third specification, *"at least two correct answers"*. The variable equals one if the respondent answered at least two of the three financial literacy questions correctly and zero, if not. The last specification was used as *"at least one correct"* which measures similarly, one if the respondent answered at least one financial literacy question correctly and zero, if not. We have used other control variables consistent with the prior research (Agnew et al., 2013; Almenberg and Säve-Söderbergh, 2011; Klapper and Panos, 2011; Lusardi and Mitchell, 2011a), such as age, gender, income, types of employment and education. We have used the dummy variable bank account as the bank to measure the impact of access to financial services. We have coded one for having a bank account and zero for not having any access to a bank account.

Table 6.4 provides the results of the first measure of financial literacy in our study to measure the impact of financial literacy on retirement planning. Logistic regression was performed, and we find that financial literacy (represented by the financial literacy score) is significant at the 5% level and essential for retirement planning in the unorganised sector in India. Results showed that financial literacy scores improve the odds of planning/willing to save for retirement by 1.35-fold. The results also highlight that males are 11.78 times more likely to save for retirement than women holding age, education, employment and income factors constant. Bank account holders are 307% (three times) more likely to save than non-bank account holders. This shows the importance of access to financial services to the working population or the overall population. Similarly, we found that income is also an important factor to the unorganised sector working population. The result showed that middle-income level workers are 79% more likely to save than higher-income workers, keeping other factors constant. Similar results are also with the educational level of the workers. It is observed that having school-level education improves the chances of savings by 1.83 times (or 183%), and higher education (graduate level/technical education) improves the same by 346% (or 3.46 times), keeping others constant. A higher level of age was significant while planning for

Table 6.4 Logistic Regression Analysis for Planning to Save with Financial Literacy Score

Dependent Variable = 1 if Willing to Save, (0, don' save)	β	S.E.	Sig.	Odd Ratio (OR)	95% CI for EXP(β)/Odd Ratio	
					Lower	Upper
FL score	0.30**	0.13	0.02	1.35	1.05	1.73
Constant	−5.95***	1.05	0.00	0.00		
Gen (1)	2.47***	0.79	0.00	11.78	2.49	55.78
Dep	0.01	0.06	0.91	1.01	0.89	1.13
Bank (1)	1.12*	0.63	0.07	3.07	0.90	10.52
Income			0.03			
Income (1)	0.58***	0.23	0.01	1.79	1.15	2.79
Income (2)	0.95	0.81	0.24	2.58	0.52	12.71
Age			0.06			
Age (1)	0.27	0.21	0.20	1.31	0.87	1.99
Age (2)	0.81**	0.35	0.02	2.25	1.14	4.42
Employ			0.42			
Employ (1)	−0.04	0.37	0.92	0.96	0.46	2.01
Employ (2)	0.25	0.31	0.42	1.28	0.70	2.33
Employ (3)	−0.63	0.74	0.39	0.53	0.13	2.26
Edu			0.01			
Edu (1)	0.60***	0.22	0.01	1.83	1.18	2.82
Edu (2)	0.12	0.29	0.68	1.13	0.64	2.00
Edu (3)	1.24**	0.60	0.04	3.46	1.06	11.29

Hosmer and Lemeshow Test: χ^2 (8) = 9.559, p = 0.298

Summary of Logistic Regression Analysis for Variables Predicting Planning to save with Financial Literacy score.
Note: ***p < 0.01; **p < 0.05; *p < 0.1.

savings, but we could not find any relation between employment types (permanent/temporary/self-employed) and plan for retirement.

We checked the goodness-of-fit test with the Hosmer–Lemeshow (H–L) test. The H–L tests the null hypothesis that predictions made by the model fit perfectly with observed group memberships. A chi-square statistic is computed comparing the observed frequencies with those expected under the linear model. A non-significant chi-square (χ^2 = 9.559, DF = 8, p = 0.298) indicates that the data fit the model well. That is, the logistic regression model was statistically significant, and the model correctly classified 73% of cases.

Summary of Logistic Regression Analysis for predicting planning to save with the second indicator (independent variable) of financial literacy, "all three correct", are presented in Table 6.5. The result shows that the "all three correct" financial literacy questions are not significant in predicting the odds of planning to save. However, all the other factors, gender (OR: 13.41, 95% CI: 2.87, 62.75), access to the bank account (OR: 3.43, 95% CI: 1.01, 11.65), middle-income level (OR: 1.87, 95% CI: 1.20, 2.91), higher age and school level education (OR; 4.19, 95% CI), are statistically significant. We found that higher education (graduate level/technical education) increased the odds of savings by 4.13 times (OR: 4.19, 95% CI: 1.30, 13.50).

When we have used the third predictor variable of financial literacy with "at least two correct" answers to predict the planning to save, we find it is statistically significant at a 1% level in predicting the odds of willing to save. Financial literacy knowledge with at least two correct answers improves the odds of saving for retirement by 1.83 times or 183%. The other control variables, such as gender, are also significant

Table 6.5 Logistic Regression Analysis for Planning to Save with Financial Literacy

Dependent Variable=1 if Willing to Save, (0, don't save)	β	S.E.	Sig.	Odd Ratio (OR)	95% CI for EXP(β)/Odd Ratio	
					Lower	Upper
All three correct	0.01	0.26	0.98	1.01	0.61	1.67
Constant	−5.65***	1.03	0.00	0.00		
Gen(1)	2.60***	0.79	0.00	13.41	2.87	62.75
Dep	0.00	0.06	0.96	1.00	0.89	1.12
Bank(1)	1.23**	0.62	0.05	3.43	1.01	11.65
Income			0.02			
Income (1)	0.63***	0.23	0.01	1.87	1.20	2.91
Income (2)	0.98	0.80	0.22	2.67	0.55	12.93
Age			0.08			
Age (1)	0.26	0.21	0.21	1.30	0.86	1.96
Age (2)	0.75**	0.34	0.03	2.12	1.08	4.15
Employ			0.45			
Employ (1)	−0.07	0.37	0.85	0.93	0.45	1.93
Employ (2)	0.19	0.31	0.54	1.21	0.66	2.20
Employ (3)	−0.72	0.73	0.32	0.49	0.12	2.04
Edu			0.00			
Edu (1)	0.66***	0.22	0.00	1.94	1.26	2.99
Edu (2)	0.29	0.29	0.31	1.34	0.76	2.36
Edu (3)	1.43**	0.60	0.02	4.19	1.30	13.50
Hosmer and Lemeshow Test: $\chi 2$ (8) = 3.967, p = 0 .860						

Summary of Logistic Regression Analysis for Variables Predicting "Planning to save" with "All three correct".
Note: ***$p < 0.01$; **$p < 0.05$; *$p < 0.1$

at a 1% significance level. It is found that males are 11.27 times more likely to plan for savings for retirement than women keeping age, education, employment and income factors constant. In this case, we also find that having a bank account improves the odds of saving almost by three (3) times with 95% confidence (0.86–10.11). Middle-income group workers are 178% with 95% confidence (1.14–2.78) are more likely to save for retirement than low-income group workers. Higher aged group workers are also 2.24 times more likely to plan for retirement savings than the young age group workers. We find similar results regarding the relationship between education and retirement savings. Those who are having school-level education (1.82 times) and with higher education, they are 3.57 times more likely to plan for old age savings with 95% confidence (1.11–11.46; Table 6.6). H–L test confirms

Table 6.6 Logistic Regression Analysis for Planning to Save with Financial Literacy

Dependent Variable=1 if Willing to Save, (0, don't save)	β	S.E.	Sig.	Odd Ratio (OR)	95% CI for EXP(β)/Odd Ratio	
					Lower	Upper
At least two correct	0.61***	0.21	0.00	1.83	1.22	2.75
Constant	−5.72***	1.04	0.00	0.00		
Gen (1)	2.42***	0.79	0.00	11.27	2.39	53.10
Dep	0.00	0.06	0.96	1.00	0.89	1.13
Bank (1)	1.08*	0.63	0.08	2.95	0.86	10.11
Income			0.03			
Income (1)	0.58***	0.23	0.01	1.78	1.14	2.78
Income (2)	0.94	0.83	0.26	2.56	0.51	12.90
Age			0.06			
Age (1)	0.28	0.21	0.18	1.32	0.87	2.00
Age (2)	0.81**	0.35	0.02	2.24	1.14	4.41
Employ			0.45			
Employ (1)	−0.03	0.37	0.94	0.97	0.47	2.03
Employ (2)	0.23	0.31	0.45	1.26	0.69	2.30
Employ (3)	−0.66	0.74	0.37	0.52	0.12	2.19
Edu			0.01			
Edu (1)	0.60***	0.22	0.01	1.82	1.18	2.80
Edu (2)	0.12	0.29	0.67	1.13	0.64	1.99
Edu (3)	1.27**	0.60	0.03	3.57	1.11	11.46
Hosmer and Lemeshow Test: $\chi 2$ (8) = 2.881, p = 0.942.						

Summary of Logistic Regression Analysis for Variables Predicting "Planning to save" with "At least two correct".
Note: ***$p < 0.01$; **$p < 0.05$; *$p < 0.1$.

Table 6.7 Logistic Regression Analysis for Planning to Save with Financial
         Literacy

Dependent Variable=1 if Willing to Save, (0, don't save)	β	S.E.	Sig.	Odd Ratio (OR)	95% CI for EXP(β)/Odd Ratio	
					Lower	Upper
At least one correct	1.03*	0.56	0.07	2.79	0.93	8.34
Constant	−6.55***	1.17	0.00	0.00		
Gen (1)	2.55***	0.79	0.00	12.85	2.72	60.69
Dep	0.00	0.06	0.96	1.00	0.89	1.13
Bank (1)	1.22**	0.63	0.05	3.39	0.99	11.57
Income			0.03			
Income (1)	0.60***	0.23	0.01	1.82	1.17	2.83
Income (2)	0.92	0.81	0.25	2.52	0.52	12.22
Age			0.07			
Age (1)	0.23	0.21	0.27	1.26	0.84	1.91
Age (2)	0.79**	0.34	0.02	2.20	1.12	4.32
Employ			0.49			
Employ (1)	−0.09	0.37	0.82	0.92	0.44	1.90
Employ (2)	0.18	0.30	0.54	1.20	0.66	2.19
Employ (3)	−0.66	0.74	0.37	0.52	0.12	2.21
Edu			0.00			
Edu (1)	0.66***	0.22	0.00	1.93	1.26	2.97
Edu (2)	0.27	0.28	0.33	1.31	0.76	2.29
Edu (3)	1.40**	0.59	0.02	4.06	1.27	13.00
Hosmer and Lemeshow Test: $\chi2$ (8) = 6.446, p = 0.597						

Summary of Logistic Regression Analysis for Variables Predicting "Planning to save"
with "At least one correct".
Note: ***$p < 0.01$; **$p < 0.05$; *$p < 0.1$.

that the logistic regression model was statistically significant, and the
model correctly classified 73.5% of cases.

In the last logistic model with the predictor variable "at least one
correct" answers to predict the planning to save for the old-age retirement benefit, we find that the predictor variable "at least one correct"
is statistically significant at a 10% level. The results of other control
variables are very similar to the other two statistically significant
models discussed earlier. We find that gender, bank account, middle-
income group, higher age level, school education and higher education
significantly improve the odds of savings (Table 6.7). The employment
category or types of employment are not significant in all the models.
We also found that the dependency does not impact retirement savings
decision-making of the unorganised sector workers.

Notes

1 Our preliminary sample size calculation used the margin of error at 3% to get a sample size of 1,067. At a 4% margin of error, the sample size would be 600, which is also way more than a random sample size of 385 at a 95% confidence level as described by (Israel, 1992).

2 http://mospi.nic.in/sites/default/files/press_release/PRESS%20NOTE%20SAE%2026-02-2021.pdf

3 https://pib.gov.in/PressReleasePage.aspx?PRID=1693225

4 There are three main issues with the linear probability model: (i) Can predict probability which is negative or larger than one (ii) A unit change in a regressor can induce an increase or decrease in probability larger than 1 (iii) a change in one unit in one regressor has a constant effect.

7 Discussion and Policy Recommendation

7.1 Discussion and Conclusions

Our study empirically demonstrates a relationship between financial literacy and willingness to save for retirement benefits among the unorganised sector workers in India. These findings are in line with some other works in developed countries (such as Agnew et al., 2013; Alessie et al., 2011; Almenberg and Säve-Söderbergh, 2011; Klapper and Panos, 2011; Lusardi and Mitchell, 2007; Van Rooij et al., 2011). We also find that some other socio-economic factors such as age, education, income level, gender and access to banks improve the willingness to save for retirement.

Our findings highlighted the importance of financial inclusion in achieving underdeveloped financial services such as old-age security or pension products. We found that access to banking improves the probability of retirement savings by three times. Therefore, primary access to financial services such as banking would induce more into the habit of savings for old age among the unorganised sector workers. Furthermore, this is also to bring to our notice that many of the workers are using the banking system (financial services) very recently, and the experience of accessing the banking services would make them comfortable to use other financial services more effectively in the near future.

The majority of the poor people in the unorganised sector still rely on or give more importance to the old system of social security to have bigger families or have a male child for their support in old age. Almost 75% of our respondents confirmed their dependency on the family after they retired from their regular course of work. Sometimes the workers also depend on remittances from their family members who have migrated to different places for their livelihood (Hoddinott, 1992; Lucas and Stark, 1985). Therefore, we could not find any empirical

DOI: 10.4324/9781003306573-7

relation between employment types and dependency rates to influence retirement planning savings. Empirically, we also found that males are 10–13 times more likely to save for retirement than women in India. Understandably, because we have a higher participation rate of men workers in unorganised sectors, and women are, in general, not making economic decisions in households due to their low levels of financial literacy (Figure 6.15).

We found that the higher age (55 years and above) is significantly associated with financial literacy; that is, financial literacy will improve with age, unlike some other countries where financial knowledge progresses to middle age and then begins to decline and creates a hump-shaped financial literacy line (Agarwal et al., 2009; Almenberg and Säve-Söderbergh, 2011; Lusardi and Mitchell, 2011c). However, this Indian experience of the unorganised sector workers may indicate that they eventually begin taking notice of the importance of retirement savings only after acquiring some real-life experiences or after developing some financial literacy skills relating to retirement planning. These findings are similar to the Australian experience highlighted by Agnew et al. (2013). Perhaps, because of the real-life experiences, the higher age group people (35–55 years) have answered the risk diversification question more accurately than their younger part (Figure 6.16). This Indian experience can be reaffirmed with our earlier findings that literacy among the higher age people in India is low, and the improvement in the literacy rate is relatively a new incidence after the Govt. of India initiated the Sarva Shiksha Abhiyan (SSA) (*Education for All Movement*) programme aimed at the universalisation of primary education free and compulsory to children between the ages of 6 and 14. Empirically, we found that school education and higher education are statistically significant in improving the savings for retirement. Our sample found that young workers (18–25 years) correctly answer all the financial literacy questions than those of the higher age group (55 years and above). Since young Indians are more literate, they could answer more accurately interest calculation questions than the higher-aged Indians (Table 6.2).

We found that middle-income level workers are statistically significant in driving retirement savings, keeping other factors constant. Therefore, a stable income level may impact the retirement savings decision of unorganised sector workers in India. With the economic growth, new job opportunities may help stabilise the source of income of the unorganised sector. More investments from the public and private sectors in the economy will boost job creation in the market. With the stable source of income, unorganised sector workers would be able to save some extra amount from their essential savings to save for their old-age security.

7.2 Policy Recommendation

Though the potential pension market in India is enormous, the pension market is under-developed primarily because the pension market relies on the organised sector, which employs merely 7% of the total workforce in Central and State Government Jobs. These schemes were based on the defined benefit (DB) system. However, most workers are engaged in the unorganised sector and are hardly covered under any old-age social security schemes, as discussed in previous chapters. Voluntary old-age security schemes, such as PPF, were there for decades but failed to attract the low-income people, and later they became a vehicle of tax-saving financial instruments for lower-middle-class income people. With the pension reforms in India, NPS introduced in 2004 for government employees, a new era of contributory DC pension schemes started. Later NPS was made available for general citizens of India. A similar contributory voluntary pension scheme, APY was made available in recent times, specifically for the unorganised sector in 2015. However, DB and DC failed to penetrate the pension market in India and covered only around 14% of the workforce in India.

This study attempts to understand the financial stress of unorganised sector workers and explore the financial decision-making behaviour regarding their old-age longevity risk. We tried to find out the awareness level (financial literacy) of the unorganised sector and their voluntary participation towards contributory pension schemes in India.

We find that little more than 50% of unorganised sector workers are aware of the different contributory pension plans, such as APY and PMSYM. Higher awareness is a positive sign for the development of this market in future. Nevertheless, out of such a high percent of aware people, only very few have contributed to those schemes in India.

We find that the workers from this segment are under certain financial stress and, therefore, they are unable to contribute to their old-age financial security. The main reasons for such financial stress are unstable income and lower level of income which compel them to invest in other requirements which are essential and eminent, such as education and health. Therefore, a stable source of income is essential to attract more workers into the contributory pension schemes. Again, if we can formalise more informal jobs into the formal sector with better job contracts may stabilise the source of income for the workers. As we have already mentioned, only 1.3% of unorganised sector workers are in formal jobs (Table 2.1). This brings us to the other policy reform in the legal aspect of the unorganised sector. At present, mandatory enrolment into the EPF system is necessary only for those organisations or establishments with 20 or more workers. If we can legislate to reduce the minimum requirement to 10 persons from the existing 20 persons, more unorganised workers would be under the mandatory cover of EPFO. This threshold would bring a substantial number of workers under the umbrella of the formal system of old-age security. This can be introduced first with the registered MSMEs and then pushed for all business units in India with minimum employees of ten persons. Introducing this mandatory cover to the MSMEs would bring 3.36 lakhs units under the coverage of EPFO along with almost 34 lakhs workers (Tables 5.2 and 5.3).

The level of financial illiteracy impacts negatively not only individual decisions but also society. Low levels of financial literacy are found to be correlated with unproductive spending and expensive borrowing and debt management across countries (Lusardi, 2019). Our study empirically finds that there is a positive relationship between higher financial literacy and old-age financial planning in India. The probability of old-age financial or pension planning increases by three times with a financially literate unorganised sector worker than a financially unaware worker. Therefore, we need to have a policy that encourages more financial literacy among unorganised sector workers. We may take direct financial literacy programmes to improve the financial literacy of old-age security for the unorganised sector worker. Previous research established that retirement planning behaviour changes significantly after completing a financial literacy learning module (Clark et al., 2017).

To deliver financial education, PFRDA needs to take financial literacy initiatives at a large scale to make it more effective by engaging with educational institutes, teachers, NGOs, especially those working in financial literacy, financial intermediaries targeting the unorganised sector workers. The initiatives which PFRDA has already taken have made them little aware of the names of those financial products, but they are not aware of the features of those schemes. We find that most unorganised sector workers are not planning for the old-age financial security and financial knowledge in India is poor even by low global standards. Therefore, financial literacy is pivotal for the growth of contributory pension schemes in India. In the long run, to improve overall financial education, it is crucial to introduce financial literacy at the school level as an indispensable subject precisely because it is crucial to expose budding minds to the basic concepts of compounding interest, inflation and risk diversifications before they make their own financial decision in the latter part of their lives. Financial literacy is very low among the young across the globe without differentiating the developed or developing countries. Financial literacy at the school level provides an opportunity for girls to have financial knowledge. Promoting financial literacy at the school level is more cost-effective than introducing it with other means at the later stage of life (Lusardi, 2019).

This research on the unorganised sector workers also brings out other critical socio-economic factors that positively correlate with old-age financial planning. It is observed that school education and higher education significantly improve the savings behaviour for retirement. Our study also finds that young workers (18–25 years) answer the interest calculation question more correctly than others. Therefore, we need to improve the educational level of the unorganised sector workers. Investment in school and technical education must improve the understanding of longevity and inflation risk to the unorganised sector workers.

This study finds that middle-income level workers are driving the retirement savings, keeping other factors constant. Therefore, a stable and higher income level, which is higher than the lower-income level, would foster the financial decision of pension investments of the unorganised sector workers in India. The Ministry of Labour & Employment (MoL&E) Government of India has constituted an Expert Group to recommend on fixation of Minimum Wages and National Floor Minimum Wages in June 2021.[1] The recommendation of this report may improve the income level of the unorganised sector workers which may help them come out of the present financial stress. With the increasing economic activities, new job creation in the market, especially in the MSME sector, where a little less skilled workers may be absorbed, would help the stable income of the unorganised sector. Therefore, the creation of job opportunities is essential for improving the investment in pension funds. More investments from the public and private sectors in the economy will boost the jobs created in the market. With the stable source of income, unorganised sector workers would be able to save some extra amount from their basic savings to save for their old-age security.

This research also brings out the supply side of the financial services to improve the pension savings behaviour of unorganised sector workers in India. We find that access to banking services increases the pension savings behaviour of unorganised sector workers by three times in India. Since financial inclusion improves familiarity with other financial products such as savings account, fixed deposits, loans, micro-insurance and money transfer through mobile banking, it helps build confidence among them about financial products. Therefore, improving financial inclusion by offering a bundle of financial products, including pension schemes, will help grow India's contributory pension savings.

Some indirect policy measures may also improve the unorganised sector's financial stress and improve the propensity to save for old-age security. Our study reveals that the workers are spending primarily on education and health purposes (Figure 6.10). The Covid-19 pandemic has made Indian policymakers realise that a sound health system involving public and private health is an essential economic and national security priority Out-of-pocket expenses (OOPE) in health has increased manifold in India. It is one of the highest globally, and OOPE for health increases the risk of vulnerable groups slipping into poverty. Therefore, investment is required to improve the present public healthcare system in India.

Health insurance schemes for hospitalisation are among the other social schemes that can cover the risk of catastrophic health expenditures. Therefore, the proper implementation and management of schemes such as Ayushman Bharat-Pradhan Mantri Jan Arogya Yojana (AB-PMJAY) by the central government or other health insurance programs by individual states are indispensable for this sector.

The outcome of this study encourages to take collective policy measures in different aspects of the government initiatives and policy implementations. It has required a collective response from the central and state governments to address this evolving issue of old-age financial security of such an enormous number of workers in unorganised sectors who are already or will contribute to India's GDP throughout their working age.

7.3 Future Scope of Work

Our study is based on the static unorganised workforce from MSMEs who are not migrating for jobs and working at the same place or same area. Therefore, more reassert is required to unearth the financial behaviour of the migrant workers who travel to different places for jobs. To do more studies on the migrant workforce of the unorganised sector, we need a robust database about them. Currently, there is no such record for those workers and we don't know the number of those workers (apart from some probable estimates) and their places of job. This year, the MoL&E, Government of India, has initiated the all India survey of migrant workers and decided to develop a database, including workers in the informal sector, as "National Database of Unorganised Workers" (NDUW). A robust data set would help improve the pension research, which would help build evidence-based policies to improve the pension cover of these workers in the future.

Even we need more research on financial literacy in India as we know little about this. Despite our study and existing knowledge, we know that financial literacy is very low in India compared to other countries. However, we still need to know how the financial literacy drive will impact the financial behaviour of the unorganised sector workers in India. We have inadequate knowledge about how to conduct the financial literacy drive and whom to target. Therefore, more research is required to uncover the different aspects of financial literacy for framing a financial literacy policy for India.

In the case of product design (contributory pension schemes), we also need some research and analysis to modify or re-orient the existing pension products or/and we may introduce customised pension schemes to suit better the unorganised pension requirement sector with more cost-effective management of the pension fund. Therefore, PFRDA should focus on more research to develop customised or effective pension products and an efficient pension market for the unorganised sector.

Note

1 https://pib.gov.in/PressReleseDetail.aspx?PRID=1723987.

References

Agarwal, S., Driscoll, J. C., Gabaix, X., & Laibson, D. (2009). The age of reason: Financial decisions over the life cycle and implications for regulation. Brookings Papers on Economic Activity, 40(2) Fall, 51–101.

Agarwal, S., Amromin, G., Ben-David, I., Chomsisengphet, S., and Evanoff, D. (2010). Financial literacy and financial planning: Evidence from India. https://ssrn.com/abstract=1728831; http://dx.doi.org/10.2139/ssrn.1728831

Agarwalla, S. K., Barua, S., Jacob, J., & Varma, J. R. (2012). A survey of financial literacy among students, young employees and the retired in India. Indian Institute of Management Ahmedabad, India.

Agnew, J. R., Bateman, H., & Thorp, S. (2013). Financial literacy and retirement planning in Australia. Numeracy, 6(2), Article 7.

Agnew, J. R., Szykman, L., Utkus, S. P., & Young, J. A. (2007). Literacy, trust, and 401(k) savings behavior. Boston College Center for Retirement Research Working Paper 2007-10.

Ahuja, R. (2003). Old-age income security for the poor. Economic and Political Weekly, 38(37), 3873–3875. September 13–19, 2003. https://www.jstor.org/stable/4414015.

Alessie, R., Van Rooij, M., & Lusardi, A. (2011). Financial literacy and retirement preparation in the Netherlands. Journal of Pension Economics & Finance, 10(4), 527–545.

Almenberg, J., & Säve-Söderbergh, J. (2011). Financial literacy and retirement planning in Sweden. Journal of Pension Economics & Finance, 10(4), 585–598.

Amlan, G., & Shrutikeerti, K. (2016). Factors influencing the participation in defined contribution pension scheme by the urban unorganized sector in India. Journal of Global Economics. 4: 176. doi:10.4172/2375-4389.1000176.

Arrondel, L., Debbich, M., & Savignac, F. (2013). Financial literacy and financial planning in France. Numeracy, 6(2), 1–17.

Asher, M. G. (2000). Reforming civil service pensions in selected Asian countries. Technical report, National University of Singapore.

Asher, M. (2007). Pension reforms in India; Indian Economy at 60: Performance and Prospects. Australia South Asia Research Centre, The Australian National University, 20–21. August, 2007.

Atkinson, A., & Messy, F. A. (2011). Assessing financial literacy in 12 countries: An OECD/INFE international pilot exercise. Journal of Pension Economics & Finance, 10(4), 657–665.

Barr, N. (2002). Reforming pensions: Myths, truths, and policy choices. International Social Security Review, 55, 3–36.

Beckmann, E. (2013). Financial literacy and household savings in Romania. Numeracy, 6(2).

Behrman, J., Mitchell, O. S., Soo, C., & Bravo, D. (2012). How financial literacy affects household wealth accumulation. American Economic Review: Papers & Proceedings, 102, 300–304. http://dx.doi.org/10.1257/aer.102.3.300.

Bernheim, D. (1995). Do households appreciate their financial vulnerabilities? An analysis of actions, perceptions, and public policy. In Walker, C. E., Bloomfield, M., & Thorning, M. (eds), Tax policy and economic growth. Washington, DC: American Council for Capital Formation, 1–30.

Blunch, N. -H., Canagarajah, S., & Raju, D. (2001). The informal sector revisited: A synthesis across space and time. World Bank Social Protection Discussion Paper No. 0119.

Boisclair, D., Lusardi, A., & Michaud, P. C. (2017). Financial literacy and retirement planning in Canada. Journal of Pension Economics & Finance, 16(3), 277–296.

Brown, M., & Graf, R. (2013). Financial literacy and retirement planning in Switzerland. Numeracy, 6(2), 1–23. http://dx.doi.org/10.5038/1936-4660.6.2.6.

Bucher-Koenen, T., & Lusardi, A. (2011). Financial literacy and retirement planning in Germany. Journal of Pension Economics & Finance, 10(4), 565–584.

Canagarajah, S., & Sethuraman, S. V. (2001). Social protection and the informal sector in developing countries: Challenges and opportunities. Social Protection Discussion Paper No. 0130. The World Bank.

Castells, M. (1996). The information age (Vol. 98). Oxford: Oxford, Blackwell Publishers.

Charmes, J. (1999a). Informal sector, poverty, and gender. A review of empirical evidence. Background paper for the World Development Report 2001. Washington, DC: The World Bank.

Charmes, J. (1999b). Gender and informal sector, contribution to The World's Women 2000, Trends and Statistics. New York: United Nations.

Chen, H., & Volpe, R. P. (1998). An analysis of personal financial literacy among college students. Financial Services Review, 7(2), 107–128.

Clark, R., Lusardi, A., & Mitchell, O. S. (2017). Employee financial literacy and retirement plan behavior: A case study. Economic Inquiry, Western Economic Association International, 55(1), 248–259.

Cochran, W. G. (1977). Sampling techniques (3rd Ed). New York: John Wiley & Sons, Inc.

CMIE. (2021). Economicoutlook. [online] Available at: https://economicoutlook. cmie.com/ [Accessed on 14.06.2021].

Cole, S., Sampson, T., & Zia, B. (2011). Prices or knowledge? What drives demand for financial services in emerging markets? Journal of Finance, 66(6), 1933–1967.

Crossan, D., Feslier, D., & Hurnard, R. (2011). Financial literacy and retirement planning in New Zealand. Journal of Pension Economics & Finance, 10(4), 619–635.

Dave, S. (2006). India's pension reform: A case study in complex institutional change. Documenting reforms: Case studies from India. January, Chairman, CMIE, Bombay. Available at: https://www.pinboxsolutions. com/wp-content/themes/PinBox/pdf/papers/Dave2006_PensionSaga. pdf.

Fornero, E., & Monticone, C. (2011). Financial literacy and pension plan participation in Italy. Journal of Pension Economics & Finance, 10(4), 547–564.

Gale, W. G., Holmes, S. E., & John, D. C. (2020). Retirement plans for contingent workers:

ILO. (2018). Women and Men in the Informal Economy: A Statistical Picture, Third Edition, Geneva: International Labour Office.

Issues and options. Journal of Pension Economics & Finance, 19(2), 185–197.

Goswami, R. (2001). Indian pension system: Problems and prognosis. Paper presented in the IAA Pensions Seminar, Brighton.

Government of India. (2004). Report of the advisory committee to advise on the administered interest rates and rationalization of savings instruments, Mumbai, January.

Hoddinott, J. (1992) Rotten kids or manipulative parents: Are children old-age security in Western Kenya? Economic Development and Cultural Change, 40, 545–566.

Holzmann, R., Packard, T., & Cuesta, J. (2000). Extending coverage in multi-pillar pension systems: Constraints and hypotheses, preliminary evidence and future research agenda. World Bank Social Protection Discussion Paper No. 0002.

Iarossi, G. (2006). The power of survey design: A user's guide for managing surveys, interpreting results, and influencing respondents. Washington, DC: The World Bank.

ILO. (2018). Women and men in the informal economy: A statistical picture (3rd Ed). Geneva: International Labour Office.

INFE, O. (2011). Measuring financial literacy: Questionnaire and guidance notes for conducting an internationally comparable survey of financial literacy. Periodical Measuring Financial Literacy: Questionnaire and Guidance Notes for conducting an Internationally Comparable Survey of Financial Literacy.

Ingham, B., Chirijevskis, A., & Carmichael, F. (2009). Implications of an increasing old-age dependency ratio: The UK and Latvian experiences compared. Pensions: An International Journal, 14, 221–230.

Irudaya Rajan, S. (Ed.) (2008). Social security for the elderly—Experiences from South Asia. London: Routledge.

Israel, G. D. (1992). Sampling the evidence of extension program impact. Program Evaluation and Organizational Development, IFAS, University of Florida. PEOD-5. October.

Kaiser, T., and Menkhoff, L. (2016). Does financial education impact financial literacy and financial behavior, and if so, when?, No 1562, Discussion Papers of DIW Berlin, DIW Berlin, German Institute for Economic Research, https://EconPapers.repec.org/RePEc:diw:diwwpp:dp1562.

Kalmi, P., & Ruuskanen, O. P. (2017). Financial literacy and retirement planning in Finland. Journal of Pension Economics & Finance, 17(3), 1–28.

Kalyani, M. (2015). Unorganised workers: A core strength of Indian labour force: An analysis. International Journal of Research, 2(12), 44–56.

Kelles-Viitanen, A. (1998). Social security for unorganized women workers. In van Ginneken, W. (ed), Social security for all Indians. New Delhi: Oxford University Press, 115–130.

Klapper, L., Lusardi, A., & Oudheusden, P. V. (2014). Financial literacy around the world: Insights from the standard & poor's ratings services Global Financial Literacy Survey. World Bank Development Research Group. www.finlit.mhfi.com.

Klapper, L., & Panos, G. A. (2011). Financial literacy and retirement planning: the Russian case. Journal of Pension Economics & Finance, 10(4), 599–618.

Kulkarni, S., Raju, S., & Smita, B. (2018). Social security for the elderly in India, an UNFPA/ISEC/IEG/TISS Project on BKBPAI: Increased awareness, access and quality of elderly services. https://india.unfpa.org/. [Accessed on 25.05.2021].

Lucas, E. B., & Stark, O. (1985). Motivations to remit: Evidence from Botswana. Journal of Political Economy, 93, 901–918.

Lusardi, A. (1999). Information, expectations, and savings for retirement. In Aaron, H. (ed), Behavioral dimensions of retirement economics. Washington, DC: Brookings Institution and Russell Sage Foundation, 81–115.

Lusardi, A. (2008). Financial literacy: An essential tool for informed consumer choice? (No. w14084). National Bureau of Economic Research.

Lusardi, A. (2009). U.S. household savings behavior: The role of financial literacy, information and financial education programs. In Foote, C., Goette, L., & Meier, S. (eds), Policymaking insights from behavioral economics. Boston, MA: Federal Reserve Bank of Boston, 109–149.

Lusardi, A. (2019). Financial literacy and the need for financial education: Evidence and implications. Swiss Journal of Economics and Statistics, 155, 1. https://doi.org/10.1186/s41937-019-0027-5.

Lusardi, A., & Beeler, J. (2007). Saving between cohorts: The role of planning. In Madrian, B., Mitchell, O., & Soldo. B. (eds), Redefining retirement: How will boomers fare? Oxford: Oxford University Press, 271–295.

Lusardi, A., & Mitchell, O. (2007). Baby boomer retirement security: The role of planning, financial literacy, and housing wealth. Journal of Monetary Economics, 54, 205–224.

Lusardi, A., & Mitchell, O. (2008). Planning and financial literacy: How do women fare? American Economic Review, 98, 413–417.

Lusardi, A., & Mitchell, O. S. (2010). How ordinary consumers make complex economic decisions: Financial literacy and retirement readiness. NBER Working Paper w15350, National Bureau of Economic Research, Cambridge, MA.

Lusardi, A., & Mitchell, O. S. (2011a). Financial literacy and planning: Implications for retirement wellbeing. In Lusardi, A., & Mitchell, O. S. (eds), Financial literacy: Implications for retirement security and the financial marketplace. Oxford, UK: Oxford University Press, 17–39. http://dx.doi.org/10.1093/acprof:oso/9780199696819.003.0002.

Lusardi, A., & Mitchell, O. S. (2011b). Financial literacy and retirement planning in the United States. Journal of Pension Economics and Finance, 10, 509–525. http://dx.doi.org/10.1017/S147474721100045X.

Lusardi, A., & Mitchell, O. S. (2011c). Financial literacy around the world: An overview. Journal of Pension Economics and Finance, 10, 497–508. http://dx.doi.org/10.1017/S1474747211000448.

Lusardi, A., & Mitchell, O. S. (2014). The economic importance of financial literacy: Theory and evidence. Journal of Economic Literature, 52(1), 5–44. http://dx.doi.org/10.1257/jel.52.1.5.

Lusardi, A., & Mitchelli, O. S. (2007). Financial literacy and retirement preparedness: Evidence and implications for financial education. Business Economics, 42(1), 35–44.

Lusardi, A., Michaud, P. -C., & Mitchell, O. S. (2013). Optimal financial knowledge and wealth inequality. National Bureau of Economic Research Working Paper 18669.

MCGPI. (2020). Mercer CFA Institute Global Pension Index, Mercer, Melbourne, Australia. Available at: https://www.mercer.com.au/our-thinking/global-pension-index.html [Accessed on 25.05.2021].

Ministry of Finance. (2019). Indian Public Finance Statistics 2017–2018. Department of Economic Affairs, Economic Division, MoF, Government of India, New Delhi.

Ministry of Finance. (2020). Pension, Demand No. 37, Note on demands for grants, Budget document 2019–2020. Ministry of Finance, Government of India.

Ministry of Finance. (2021). Economic Survey 2020-21, Government of India. https://www.indiabudget.gov.in/budget2021-22/economicsurvey/index.php.

Ministry of Labour & Employment (MoL&E). (2015). Report on employment in informal sector and conditions of informal employment, Labour Bureau, Government of India, Chandigarh, India.

Ministry of Micro, Small & Medium Enterprises (MoMSME). (2021). Annual report, 2020–21.

Ministry of Statistics and Programme Implementation (MoSPI). (2020). Periodic Labour Force Survey (PLFS), Government of India, New Delhi.

Mitchell, O. S., & Lusardi, A. (2015). Financial literacy and economic outcomes: Evidence and policy implications. The Journal of Retirement, 3(1), 107–114.

Moure, N. G. (2016). Financial literacy and retirement planning in Chile. Journal of Pension Economics & Finance, 15(2), 203–223.

Murthy, S. V. R. (2019). Measuring informal economy in India: Indian experience, 7th IMF Statistical Forum: Measuring the Informal Economy, IMF, Washington, DC.

NCEUS. (2007). Report on conditions of work and promotion of livelihoods in the unorganised sector. New Delhi: Academic Foundation.

NCEUS. (2009). The Challenge of Employment: An Informal Economy Perspective. New Delhi: Academic Foundation

NSAP. (2021). National social assistance programme. [online] Available at: https://nsap.nic.in/.

NSC (2012). Report of the Committee on Unorganised Sector Statistics. New Delhi: Government of India. http://hdl.handle.net/123456789/2848.

OECD. (2017). G20/OECD INFE report on adult financial literacy in G20 countries.

Palacios, R., & Sane, R. (2013). Learning from the early experience of India's matching defined contribution scheme. In Hinz, R., Holzmann, R., Tuesta, D., & Takayama, N. (ed), Matching contributions for pensions: A review of international experience. Washington, DC: The World Bank.

PFRDA. (2020). Annual Report 2019–2020. New Delhi: PFRDA. www.pfrda.or.in.

PFRDA (2021). Annual Report 2020-2021. New Delhi: PFRDA. www.pfrda.or.in

Planning Commission. (2001). Report of working group on Social Security. Planning Commission, Govt. of India, New Delhi.

Planning Commission. (2006). Report of working group on Social Security. Planning Commission, Govt. of India, New Delhi.

Poterba, J. M., Venti, S. F., & Wise, D. A. (2013). Health, education, and the post-retirement evolution of household assets. National Bureau of Economic Research Working Paper 18695.

Rajsekhar, D., Keshavan, S., & Manjula, R. (2016). Contributory pension schemes for the poor: Issues and ways forward. Working Paper 377. The Institute for Social and Economic Change, Bangalore, India.

Rajesh. (2021). Labour Welfare Fund State Wise 2021 in India, HR Cabin. https://www.hrcabin.com/labour-welfare-fund-state-wise-in-india/

Sane, R., & Thomas, S. (2014). The way forward for India's National Pension System. WP-2014-022, Indira Gandhi Institute of Development Research,

Mumbai. Available at: http://www.igidr.ac.in/pdf/publication/WP-2014-022.pdf.

Sanyal, A., & Singh, C. (2013). Universal pension scheme in India. Working Paper No. 420. IIM Bangalore, Bangaluru, India.

Sarva Shiksha Abhiyan. Department of School Education and Literacy, MHRD, Government of India. https://samagra.education.gov.in/.

Sekita, S. (2011). Financial literacy and retirement planning in Japan. Journal of Pension Economics and Finance, 10(4), 637–656.

Sethuraman, S. V. (1997). Urban poverty and the informal sector: A critical assessment of current strategies. ILO.

Shankar, S., & Asher, M. (2011). Micro-pensions in India: Issues and challenges. International Social Security Review, 64. doi: 10.1111/j.1468-246X.2011.01390.x.

Stango, V., and Zinman, J. (2007). Fuzzy Math and red ink: When the opportunity cost of consumption is not what it seems. Dartmouth College, Working Paper.

The Government of India. (2000). The project Old Age Social and Income Security (OASIS) report. New Delhi: Ministry of Social Justice and Empowerment, Government of India.

The National Commission for Enterprises in the Unorganized Sector. (2009). The challenge of employment in India: An informal economy perspective (Vol. 1). New Delhi: Academic Foundation.

The Unorganised Workers' Social Security Act (UWSSA). (2009). Vide notification no. S.O. 1220(E), dated 14th May, 2009, Gazette of India, Extraordinary, Part II, sec. 3 (ii), Government of India. https://legislative.gov.in/sites/default/files/A2008-33.pdf.

United Nations Population Fund (UNFPA). (2012a). UNFPA working Paper Series 7. New Delhi: UNFPA.

United Nations Population Fund (UNFPA). (2012b). Ageing in twenty first century: A celebration and a challenge. New York. www.unfpa.org.

United Nations. (2019). World population prospect. DESA, population division. [online] Available at: https://population.un.org/wpp/ [Accessed on 14.06.2021].

van Rooij, M., Lusardi, A., and Alessie, R.J.M. (2007). Financial literacy and stock market participation. DNB Working Paper No. 146, Michigan Retirement Research Center Research Paper No. 2007-162. https://ssrn.com/abstract=1014994

Van Rooij, M., Lusardi, A., & Alessie, R. (2011). Financial literacy and stock market participation. Journal of Financial Economics, 101(2), 449–472.

Van Rooij, M., Lusardi, A., & Alessie, R. (2012). Financial literacy, retirement planning and household wealth. Economic Journal, 122(560), 449–478.

Warwick, D. P., & Lininger, C. A. (1975). The sample survey: Theory and practice. New York: McGraw-Hill.

Willmore, L. (2000). Three pillars of pensions? A proposal to end mandatory contributions; Discission Paper of the United Nations Department of Economic and Social Affairs, Paper No. 13, United Nations. Available at: https://www.un.org/esa/esa00dp13.pdf.

World Bank. (1994). Averting the old-age crisis: Policies to protect the old and promote growth. Washington DC.

Annexure 1
The Questionnaire

1. Name: 2   Address:

3. Gender: ☐ Male   ☐ Female   ☐ Transgender

4. Age (years): ☐ 18–25   ☐ 26–35   ☐ 36–45   ☐ 46–55
                ☐ 56–65   ☐ 66–75   ☐ >75

5. Religion:
   ☐ Hindu   ☐ Muslim   ☐ Christians   ☐ Buddhist
   ☐ Shik   ☐ Jain Other(_____)

6. Marital Status: ☐ Married   ☐ Unmarried   ☐ Widow
                      ☐ Divorced   ☐ Separated

7. Literacy (Education):
   ☐ Illiterate   ☐ <=V   ☐ <=VII   ☐ <=X   ☐ <=XII
   ☐ <=UG or <=PG

8. Occupation: _____ (Farmer/ Artisan/ Auto
   or Van Driver/ Taxi driver/ Rickshaw puller/ Potter/ Load
   carrier/ Railway station Coolie/ Domestic help/Small and
   marginal farmers/landless agricultural laborers/fishermen/ Vegetable Vendors/leather workers/ weavers/those engaged in animal
   husbandry/Beedi rolling/ Labelling and packing/ building and
   construction / Brick kilns and stone quarries/sawmills/ oil mills/
   Tea stall vendors)

9. Nature of Employment:
   ☐ Permanent   ☐ Temporary(Contractual)   ☐ Self employed
   ☐ Daily Paid ☐ Other(_____)

10. Number of family members (Family Size): _____

11. Number of dependent family members: _____

12. Monthly Income: (Rs. In Thousands)
    - ☐ <5k   ☐ 5k–10k   ☐ 10k–15k   ☐ 15k–20k
    - ☐ 20k–25k   ☐ 25k–30k   ☐ 30k–35k   ☐ >35k

13. How much is your monthly expense: (Rs. In thousands (k))
    - ☐ <5k   ☐ 5k–10k   ☐ 10k–15k   ☐ 15k–20k
    - ☐ 20k–25k   ☐ 25k–30k   ☐ 30k–35k   ☐ >35k

14. Do you have a bank account: ☐ Yes   ☐ No

15. Does any of your family member have a bank account:
    ☐ Yes   ☐ No

16. Does any of your family member invest: ☐ Yes   ☐ No

17. How much are you able to save (Monthly): ☐ Do not save
    ☐ Rs. _____ (If No then go to Q No. 20)

18. Purpose of savings:
    - ☐ Domestic purpose (Buying property or real estates/construction/ repair/ renovation)
    - ☐ Healthcare
    - ☐ Child Education
    - ☐ Old age security (Retirement)
    - ☐ Child marriage
    - ☐ Others: _____

19. Mode of saving:
    - ☐ Liquid asset (cash in hand)   ☐ Buying Property
    - ☐ Bank A/c   ☐ Buying pension scheme/ welfare scheme
    - ☐ Post office   ☐ Invest in stock market
    - ☐ Life Insurance   ☐ PPF
    - ☐ Buying Gold/metal   ☐ Others: _____

20. Have you ever tried to know how much you need to save for retirement? ☐ Yes   ☐ No   ☐ Do not know

21. Tell me about the ways you tried to know how much your household would need at the time of retirement?
    - ☐ Talk to your family and relatives
    - ☐ Talk to your co-workers and friend
    - ☐ Talk to your union/community leader
    - ☐ Talk to Bank
    - ☐ Consult a financial planner or investment advisor or an accountant
    - ☐ Others:

22. How often do you keep track of your actual spending?
☐ Always   ☐ Mostly   ☐ Rarely   ☐ Never

23. Do you have any plan for your retirement savings: ☐ Yes   ☐ No

24. Have you heard about
☐ PMSYM   ☐ APY/ Swavalamban Yojana   ☐ None
*PMSYM: Pradhan Mantri Shram Yogi Maan-Dhan scheme
*APY: Atal Pension Yojana

25. How did you hear about the scheme?
☐ TV advertisement   ☐ Hoarding
☐ Radio   ☐ Community gathering
☐ Co-worker   ☐ Others: _____

26. How do you save for the retirement:
☐ Invested in Pension/Welfare Plan   ☐ Invested in Gold
☐ Invested in Land/ property   ☐ Saving in Bank A/C
☐ Liquid cash (cash in hand)
☐ Does have other business plans
☐ Income from leasing and selling properties
☐ PPF   ☐ Others: _____

27. Are you investing in any kind of government retirement scheme:
☐ Yes   ☐ No

28. Are you investing in any kind of private retirement scheme:
☐ Yes   ☐ No

29. Do you have any farmland or land or any other kind of asset in native place: ☐ Yes   ☐ No

30. Are you covered by any Government scheme: (widow pension scheme/ health pension scheme/welfare scheme): ☐ No
☐ Kanyashree   ☐ Swastha Sathi   ☐ Others: _____

31. Do you have any debt or loan: ☐ Yes   ☐ No

32. Will you be dependent on your family members after retirement:
☐ Yes   ☐ No

33. Suppose you get a lottery of Rs. 50,000 how would you use the money
    - ☐ Personal need (repair house/ buy something....) Rs _____
    - ☐ Repay my loan Rs _____
    - ☐ Start my business Rs _____
    - ☐ Buy Gold/ Silver/ Metal Rs _____
    - ☐ Buy some retirement scheme/welfare scheme Rs _____
    - ☐ Deposit in bank Rs _____
    - ☐ Deposit in Post Office Rs _____
    - ☐ Buy land/Property Rs _____
    - ☐ Other _____ Rs _____

34. Calculation of interest plus principle: Suppose you put Rs. 1,000 into a savings account with a guaranteed interest rate of 4% per year. How much would be in the account at the end of the first year, once the interest payment is made? [Open response: correct answer Rs. 1,040]
    Rs. _____

35. Suppose you have Rs. 200 in a savings account and the interest is 10% per year. How much will you have in the account after two years? (Amount in Rs)
    - ☐ Exactly 220   ☐ Exactly 240   ☐ Less than 240
    - ☐ More than 240   ☐ Do Not Know

36. Definition of Inflation: High Inflation means cost of living is increasing rapidly?   ☐ True   ☐ False

37. Suppose that in the year 2020, your income has doubled and prices of all goods have doubled too. In 2020, how much will you be able to buy with your income?
    - ☐ More than today   ☐ Exactly the same ☐ Less than today
    - ☐ Do not know   ☐ Refuse to

38. You have two investment opportunities to invest Rs. 10,000
    a) Invest in a private company for three years which will get an expected return of Rs. 30,000.
    b) Invest in a bank as fixed deposit at a rate of 10% for three years which will return of Rs. 13,310 Which one you wish to invest?
       ☐ (a)   ☐ (b)   ☐ None

39. Assume a friend inherits Rs. 10,000 today and his sibling inherits Rs. 10,000, three years from now. Who is richer because of the inheritance?

☐ My friend   ☐ His sibling   ☐ They are equally rich
☐ Do not know   ☐ Refuse to ans

40. An investment with a high return is likely to be high risk?

☐ True   ☐ False   ☐ Do not Know

41. It is less likely that you will lose all of your money if you save it in more than one place

☐ Yes   ☐ No

42. What do you think about present economic condition of India?

☐ Very Good   ☐ Good   ☐ Bad   ☐ Very Bad
☐ Does Not Understand Other Response

Annexure 2

Distribution of Responses to Financial Literacy by Age, Gender, Education and Employment Status with All Four Questions (%)

	Interest		Inflation		Time Value of Money		Risk Diversification		Overall 4 Measures		n
	Correct	Incorrect	Correct	Incorrect	Correct	Incorrect	Correct	Incorrect	All Correct	At Least 1 Correct	
Education											
Up to class VII	18.20	81.79	55.67	44.32	51.45	48.54	78.36	21.63	7.12	93.93	379
Up to class X	40.24	59.75	58.53	41.46	55.48	44.51	76.82	23.17	10.97	97.56	164
Up to class XII	60.67	39.32	71.91	28.08	60.67	39.32	79.77	20.22	23.59	96.62	89
Graduation and above	52.38	47.61	60	40	61.90	38.09	80.95	19.04	28.57	90.47	21
Gender											
Male	32.22	67.77	61.64	38.35	57.44	42.55	78.80	21.19	11.38	95.97	571
Female	19.51	80.48	37.80	62.19	30.48	69.51	74.39	25.60	8.53	89.02	82
Age											
18–25 years	40.78	59.21	48.68	51.31	51.31	48.68	75	25	13.15	92.10	76
26–35 years	36	64	62.85	37.14	52	48	76	24	13.71	94.85	175
36–45 years	27.44	72.55	58.60	41.39	54.41	45.58	80.93	19.06	8.37	95.34	215
46–55 years	27.40	72.59	56.29	43.70	57.03	42.96	81.48	18.51	11.85	97.03	135
55 years above	19	80.76	65.38	34.61	55.76	44.23	71.15	28.84	7.69	94.23	52
Employment Status											
Permanent	33.67	66.32	60.20	39.79	55.10	44.89	77.55	22.44	15.30	94.89	98
Temporary (contractual)	29.88	70.11	59.76	40.23	55.76	44.23	78.11	21.88	8.70	96	425
Self employed	29.16	70.83	39.58	60.41	35.41	64.58	72.91	27.08	16.66	85.41	48
Daily paid	31.70	68.29	62.19	37.80	54.87	45.12	82.92	17.07	14.63	96.34	82

Compiled from the sample collected through the survey.

Annexure 3

Demographic Characteristics of Sample Respondents

Sl no.	Variables	Percentage of Sample
1	Gender	
	male	87.44
	female	12.55
2	Marital status	
	Married	80.09
	Unmarried	18.98
	Widow	0.30
	Divorced	0.30
	Separated	0.30
3	Level of education	
	Up to class 8	58.03
	Up to class 10	25.11
	Up to class 12	13.62
	Graduation and above	3.21
4	Income	
	Below 5k	4.44
	5k–10k	25.42
	10k–15k	51.76
	15k–20k	16.38
	Above 20k	1.99
5	Age	
	18–25 years	11.63
	26–35 years	26.79
	36–45 years	32.92
	46–55 years	20.67
	55 years above	7.96

Compiled from the sample collected through the survey.

Index

Note: **Bold** page numbers refer to tables; *italic* page numbers refer to figures and page numbers followed by "n" denote endnotes.